Volume VI
Report No. 62
June, 1966

Psychopathological Disorders in Childhood: Theoretical Considerations and a Proposed Classification

Formulated by the
Committee on Child Psychiatry

Group for the Advancement of Psychiatry

Additional copies of this GAP Report No. 62 are available at the following prices: 1-9 copies, $4.00 each; 10-24 copies, list less 15 per cent; 25-99 copies, list less 20 per cent; 100-499 copies, list less 30 per cent.

Upon request the Publications Office of the Group for the Advancement of Psychiatry will provide a complete listing of GAP titles currently in print, quantity prices, and information on subscriptions assuring the receipt of new publications as they are released.

Bound volumes of Reports and Symposiums published since 1947 are also available. They include GAP publications no longer in print that are unavailable in any other form.

Orders amounting to less than $5.00 must be accompanied by remittance. All prices are subject to change without notice.

Please send your order and remittance to: Publications Office, Group for the Advancement of Psychiatry, 419 Park Avenue South, New York, New York 10016.

Standard Book Number 87318-098-4

Library of Congress Catalog Card Number 62-2872

Printed in the United States of America

SIXTH PRINTING, *December 1973*

Table of Contents

This report is the third in a series of Reports and Symposiums that will comprise Volume VI. For a list of other GAP publications on topics related to the subject of this report, please see page 346.

STATEMENT OF PURPOSE

The GROUP FOR THE ADVANCEMENT OF PSYCHIATRY has a membership of approximately 185 psychiatrists, organized in the form of a number of working committees which direct their efforts toward the study of various aspects of psychiatry and toward the application of this knowledge to the fields of mental health and human relations.

Collaboration with specialists in other disciplines has been and is one of GAP's working principles. Since the formation of GAP in 1946 its members have worked closely with such other specialists as anthropologists, biologists, economists, statisticians, educators, lawyers, nurses, psychologists, sociologists, social workers, and experts in mass communication, philosophy, and semantics. GAP envisages a continuing program of work according to the following aims:

1. To collect and appraise significant data in the field of psychiatry, mental health, and human relations;
2. To reevaluate old concepts and to develop and test new ones;
3. To apply the knowledge thus obtained for the promotion of mental health in good human relations.

GAP is an independent group and its reports represent the composite findings and opinions of its members only, guided by its many consultants.

PSYCHOPATHOLOGICAL DISORDERS IN CHILDHOOD: THEORETICAL CONSIDERATIONS AND A PROPOSED CLASSIFICATION *was formulated by the Committee on Child Psychiatry.* The members of this Committee as well as all other Committees are listed below.

---

* At the time this report was formulated by the Committee on Child Psychiatry, it was under the chairmanship of Dane G. Prugh. The present members of the Committee wish to express their indebtedness to former members, a number of whom were involved, directly or indirectly, in the development of the ideas set forth herein. Those directly involved include Anna R. Benjamin, Leon Eisenberg, George E. Gardner, Othilda Krug, Reginald S. Lourie, Eleanor Pavenstedt, Eveoleen N. Rexford, and J. Franklin Robinson. Dr. Stella Chess rendered valuable assistance to the Committee as a consultant.

INTRODUCTION

*"Do you mean you think you can find the answer to it?" said
the March Hare. "Exactly so," said Alice. "Then you should
say what you mean," the March Hare went on. "I do," Alice
hastily replied; "at least I mean what I say—that's the same
thing, you know." "Not the same thing a bit," said the mad
Hatter.
"Oh well! It means much the same thing," said the Duchess. . . . ,
"and the moral of that is—'take care of the sense and the sounds
will take care of themselves.' "*

Lewis Carroll, *Alice in Wonderland*

The need for a more adequate and useful classification dealing
with disorders of mental and emotional nature in children and
adolescents has long been recognized by child and adult psychiatrists. The Committee on Child Psychiatry of the Group for the
Advancement of Psychiatry has been concerned with this matter
for a number of years, as have other groups of professional
workers. In a previous publication, THE DIAGNOSTIC PROCESS IN
CHILD PSYCHIATRY,[1] the urgency of the need for such a classification was pointed out, and for the past several years the Committee has addressed itself specifically to this issue.

The task has been a challenging and a humbling one. As yet,
no all-encompassing, unequivocally accepted conceptual framework exists within which the intricate interrelationships among
somatic, intellectual, emotional and social processes and phenomena in the developing child can be comprehended and organized in
a thoroughly logical, all-inclusive fashion. Nevertheless, the Com-

173

mittee still felt that sufficient understanding and knowledge are available at this time for the development of a workable if not ideal classification.

The marked discrepancies among current nosological approaches to childhood disorders and the disparities among nomenclatural terms employed underline the need for a classification based upon explicit and clearly defined categories that can be employed by clinicians from varying conceptual backgrounds. Such categories are important for the purposes of ready communication in work and teaching, the collection of comparable data, the study of the natural history of disease pictures, the assessment of treatment outcome and prognostic outlook, and the investigation of epidemiologic factors. It is recognized that all scientific method is founded first upon careful observation, description, and classification leading to the induction of testable hypotheses and to ultimate prediction and modification of existing phenomena. The result of the Committee's labors to further the stage of classification will, it is hoped, be tried out by various clinicians in order to determine its usefulness. Individual members of the Committee from differing theoretical and experiential backgrounds have utilized the classification informally with some positive results. It remains for the larger community of clinicians to accept, reject, or modify the scheme presented.

1
HISTORICAL AND CONCEPTUAL BACKGROUND

Historical Aspects

In attempting to evolve a workable nosology, the Committee has logically turned first to the efforts of the past and to the history of scientific thought in this area. The nineteenth century scientific model of human behavior was essentially dualistic and static in nature. It was derived from the model employed by the natural scientists of that day, who tended to accept their basic assumptions as representative of absolute truths—for example the polarities of life and death, of body and soul, and of rational and irrational mind. They assumed further that scientific mastery should be absolute and should be based upon complete objectivity and logical thought. They held the belief that all phenomena could be arranged in an uncontestably hierarchical, logical order within the appropriate conceptual framework. The monumental contributions to psychiatric nosology offered by Kraepelin[2] partook of many of these characteristics of nineteenth century thought in spite of their constructive impetus toward clarity and order.

Present-day scientific developments have challenged some of the nineteenth century assumptions. The concept of polarity, the need for basic assumptions, and the use of deductive and inductive techniques have been retained. Antithetical concepts, such as rational and irrational, have been challenged by reputable scientists. In addition, we now recognize that rational, conscious mental activity cannot be sharply or totally isolated from unconscious and irrational mental processes. Mental and physiological

175

states are now seen to influence each other unavoidably and continuously. Normality and abnormality are felt to be concepts that are difficult to define, rather representing theoretical or operational constructs in a particular sociocultural and historical context than absolute and incontestable truths. In short, twentieth century scientific thinking in a number of fields strives to be multidimensional, relativistic, and dynamic in character, relying on probabilities rather than certainties.

Classification of children's disorders in this century must therefore draw upon contemporary modes of thought and understanding of human behavior and should embrace phenomenological and operational points of view. It is thus impossible to insist that a diagnostic format of today be founded upon and derived from an all-embracing and unchallengeable nosology offering absolute comparability, reliability, validity, and predictability. It is equally inconceivable to adopt an adiagnostic or aconceptual approach and simply to collect data regarding bits of behavior or symptomatology without the use of any organizing or structuring concepts. Although a phenomenologic approach is vital, it is not sufficient. Despite the limitations of our knowledge, some reordering of phenomena is necessary in terms of an overall conceptual framework. A traditional medical somatic model is inadequate in dealing with psychopathological disorders. Descriptive-clinical, genetic, and dynamic dimensions must be included in such a conceptual framework, in a manner appropriate to the developmental nature of childhood.

Previous Classifications

Before considering the setting up of such a conceptual scheme, the contributions toward classification in the past should be mentioned. Stengel[5] has admirably summarized these contributions in regard to adult disorders in his extensive review of the problems and complexities in this area. As he has indicated, difficulties arise in part from the current use of differing systems of classification in varying parts of the world, despite the existence of the International Statistical Classification of Diseases, Injuries and Causes of Death.[3] Stengel has crystallized the principle of *operational definition* upon which an ideal classification must be based. In addition, he has emphasized the difference between a nomenclature, with all its richness and necessary flexibility, and a systematic classification susceptible to statistical handling. Others have underlined the distinction between the process of diagnosis (or *knowing through*), which involves the clinical determination of disease pictures, and the act of classification, or the systematic arrangement of diseases in classes according to a method or system. Classification of any individual problem under any scheme of course rests upon thorough diagnostic study and evaluation of the nature and degree of the psychopathological processes in the particular child.

In reviewing past classifications of children's disorders, the Committee was struck with the variety of approaches by capable people, struggling, as we have struggled, with the problems of scientific philosophy and conceptualization. A number of such schemes are included in a section of the Appendix herein. These schemes are based upon strictly descriptive or phenomenological points of view in relation to behavior; currently popular concepts of etiology, ranging from somatic origins to psychogenesis; chronological or developmental perspectives; considerations regarding total versus partial personality reactions; parent-child relationships and family interactions; the degree of treatability; or, more commonly, a combination of several of these conceptual views. The complexities and fluidities of professional thought in this field have offered understandable frustrations to all those courageous persons who have put forth classifications of childhood disorders reflecting their individual points of view. Each has made some contribution to the mosaic of understanding and systematization.

The classification of adult psychiatric disorders offered by the 1961 revision of the Standard Nomenclature of Diseases and Operations[4], in the section dealing with diseases of the psychobiologic unit, has drawn upon twentieth century dynamic psychology, broadly defined, for its conceptual framework and has offered definitions of descriptive-dynamic nature for its nosological categories. Even this significant advance leaves untouched many of the developmental gradients of psychopathology in childhood and adolescence. The need remains for a separate classification dealing with childhood and adolescence, despite some overlap between the problems of the latter age group and those of adults.

Conceptual Considerations

Emboldened by its excursion into history, the Committee saw as its first task the formulation of a conceptual framework that would encompass the characteristics of personality formation and development in childhood in sufficiently comprehensive fashion to permit professional people from differing schools of thought to agree at least upon a point of departure to a classification of disturbances and deviations. The influence of hereditary factors, the impact of familial and other environmental influences, the significance of developmental capacities and vulnerabilities, the fluidity and plasticity of the young child's personality characteristics, and other considerations obviously had to be taken into account. In addition, the tendency of the clinician to see and classify pathology rather than health was recognized. Accordingly, the conceptual scheme evolved must permit in some measure an understanding and classification of healthy as well as unhealthy reactions or behaviors. Above all, such a conceptual framework must be clinically relevant, if it is to be at all helpful in undergirding a classification constructed for everyday clinical usage.

In searching for a theoretical framework that would meet the various tests it must survive, the Committee felt that three basic propositions were vital: (a) the *psychosomatic concept,* involving the unity of mind and body and the interrelatedness between psychological and somatic processes; (b) the *developmental dimension,* so central to the study of the child; and (c) the *psychosocial aspects* of the child's existence in the family and society.

Selected References

1. Group for the Advancement of Psychiatry, Committee on Child Psychiatry: THE DIAGNOSTIC PROCESS IN CHILD PSYCHIATRY, GAP Report No. *38,* August, 1957.
2. Kraepelin, E.: PSYCHIATRIE: EIN LEHRBUCH FÜR STUDIERENDE UND AERTZE, 6th ed., J. A. Barth, Leipzig, Germany, 1899.
3. MANUAL OF THE INTERNATIONAL STATISTICAL CLASSIFICATION OF DISEASES, INJURIES, AND CAUSES OF DEATH, World Health Organization, Geneva, 1957.
4. STANDARD NOMENCLATURE OF DISEASES AND OPERATIONS, 5th ed., Blakiston Division of McGraw-Hill Book Co., Inc., New York, 1961.
5. Stengel, G.: "Classification of Mental Disorders," *Bulletin of the World Health Organization* Vol. 21, 1960, pp. 601-663.

The psychosomatic concept:

The body of theory which most closely meets the need for the conceptualizations embodied in this proposition is centered on the unitary theory of health and disease. This set of theoretical constructs derives from the seminal concepts of Bernard,[1] Freud,[3] Cannon,[2] and Meyer,[7] and has been elucidated most clearly by G. Engel,[4] with important contributions by Romano,[10] Mirsky,[8] Greene,[5] and Grinker,[6] among others.[9, 11]

In this view, health and disease are considered as "phases of life." Health represents the phase of positive adaptation by the human organism and, in the child, the phase of growth and development. In this phase, the child is able to master his environment and himself, within stage-appropriate limits, and is reasonably free from pain, disability, or limitations in social capacities. Disease represents the phase of failure in adaptation or of breakdown in the attempts of the organism to maintain an adaptive equilibrium or the dynamic steady state.

The human being is seen as possessing three basic levels of organization: *physiological, psychological,* and *social* or interpersonal. Interrelationships among these levels operate at nodal points of communication among the "open systems," coordinated by the central regulating system (brain and mental apparatus) and the neuroendocrine system. Noxious stimuli from the environment, of physical or interpersonal nature, may interfere with the satisfaction of basic needs (ranging from oxygen intake to sexual expression) or they may damage or disturb in function organs or parts of the body, thus indirectly interfering with need satisfactions and with the maintenance of the dynamic steady state.

1. The Concept of Stress

Potentially stressful stimuli for the organism may be of physical, psychological, or social or interpersonal nature. *Physical stimuli*, including infectious organisms, may injure by virtue of their chemical, antigenic, or physical properties, or they may involve insufficiencies of materials inside or outside the body. They operate at a biochemical level in the organism, affecting molecules, cells, tissues, or organs; physiologic defenses or compensatory mechanisms are frequently called into play in order to maintain physiological homeostasis. *Psychologically stressful stimuli* derive from thoughts or feelings that are unacceptable to the individual or are conflict-producing by reason of past experience or the current situation. They must be registered by the perceptual systems and receive conscious or unconscious central symbolic representation in the mental apparatus. The fantasies, memories, and emotions aroused by these stimuli may lead to the evocation of various psychological defenses or compensatory behavioral devices in an attempt to achieve an individual adaptive equilibrium and to prevent psychological decompensation or adaptive breakdown. Psychological stimuli of stressful significance are closely interwoven with *social stimuli* of stressful character involving the loss or threat of loss of key relationships, the occurrence of real or fantasied danger, or the frustration of a drive or need state, as a result of particular disruptions or distortions in interpersonal relations or social role functioning. Behavioral coping devices may be utilized by the child—with differences at the various developmental levels and with varying responses from other persons—in order to maintain interpersonal adaptation or equilibrium.

Stimuli of physical, psychological, or social nature may thus impinge upon the individual, producing adaptive breakdown or disease when operating qualitatively or quantitatively in sufficient degree. Stressful stimuli are relative, not absolute. The nature and degree of the response to the impact of any noxious stimulus at any particular time are determined by *hereditary, constitutional, developmental, and experiential factors.* Thus the child's adaptive capacity is influenced by his own innate characteristics as well as by his past experience, the reactions of key persons, and, within broad limits, the degree of noxious influence of the current stimulus, plus the transactional feedbacks among all these variables. Significantly stressful stimuli may initially come into play at physiological, psychological, or social levels of organization, with reverberations taking place in systems other than the system originally affected. Disease states or states of adaptive breakdown may thus assume predominantly physical or psychological characteristics, depending upon the point of initial impingement of the particular stressful stimuli and upon the adaptive response of the organism.

2. Disease Pictures

If the major stressful stimuli are predominantly of physical nature, the resulting changes in physiologic systems may bring about transactional reverberations at the psychological or social levels of organization, often bringing into play psychological defenses or social adaptive devices. Secondary reverberations may occur "back" upon the physiological level, affecting systems other than those originally involved. If psychological or social stressful stimuli occur that result in emotional conflict, the signal anxiety called out in the ego, indicating impending disruption of the dynamic steady state, may evoke initially psychological defenses or social adaptive devices. If conflict and "unpleasant" emotions persist, physiologic concomitants of the emotions remain. The latter are ordinarily reversible with resolution of the emotional conflict and diminution of the signal anxiety. If conflict persists, however, these physiologic concomitants may exert a strain upon the physiologic capacities of the child, as with an already damaged heart; they may also precipitate or enhance pre-existing or latent pathological processes at the biochemical or organ system levels, producing what are currently designated as psychophysiological disorders. These disorders may in turn directly affect the mental apparatus, as in diabetic coma, or they may arouse further psychological defenses or social adaptive devices, with their answering reactions on the part of parents and family members to the presence of illness or disability. Failures in such adaptive maneuvers may lead to inappropriate usage of psychological defenses, producing further decompensation, as in the child who denies the presence of diabetes and overeats.

In individuals predisposed experientially and (presumably) constitutionally, the persistence of emotional conflict may lead to unhealthy and maladaptive extremes in the attempt to employ psychological defenses or social maneuvers. Thus may be produced the clinical pictures known as psychoneuroses, personality or character disorders, or psychoses, the psychoses representing extreme psychological decompensation or adaptive breakdown.

From this point of view, the signs or symptoms of any disease state, in addition to the direct effects of the stressful stimulus, may also be determined less directly by the child's attempts to maintain adaptation or by the results of the adaptive outcome. Examples would range from the variations in the immunity of the host to tuberculosis, to the variability of the effects of direct insult to the central nervous system, depending upon the social, educational, and other demands made upon the child.

In the process of diagnostic evaluation, the clinician thus undertakes a positive weighting of the relevant physical and psychological and social factors involved, including the forces of health. While avoiding a dichotomy between wholly physical, or organic, and completely psychological, or functional, concepts of disease, he may arrive at an arbitrary designation of predominantly physical or predominantly psychological disease states for the purposes of classification, without neglecting either set of factors in his diagnostic formulation.

Selected References

1. Bernard, C.: AN INTRODUCTION TO THE STUDY OF EXPERIMENTAL MEDICINE, The Macmillan Co., Inc., New York, 1927.
2. Cannon, W. B.: THE WISDOM OF THE BODY, W. W. Norton & Co., Inc., New York, 1932.
3. Engel, G. L.: "A Unified Concept of Health and Disease." *Perspectives in Biology and Medicine,* Vol. 3, 1960, p. 459.
4. Freud, S.: AN OUTLINE OF PSYCHOANALYSIS, W. W. Norton & Co., Inc., New York, 1940.
5. Greene, W. A.: "Process in Psychosomatic Disorders," *Psychosomatic Medicine,* Vol. 28, 1956, p. 150.
6. Grinker, R. R., ed.: TOWARD A UNITARY THEORY OF HUMAN BEHAVIOR, Basic Books, Inc., New York, 1959.
7. Meyer, A.: "Objective Psychology or Psychobiology, with Subordination of the Medically Useless Contrast of Mental and Physical," *Journal of the American Medical Association* Vol. 65, 1915, p. 860.
8. Mirsky, I. A.: "Physiologic, Psychologic, and Social Determinants of Psychosomatic Disorders," *Diseases of the Nervous System,* Vol. 21, 1960, p. 50.
9. Prugh, D. G.: "Toward an Understanding of Psychosomatic Concepts in Relation to Illness in Childhood," in A. Solnit and S. Provence, eds., MODERN PERSPECTIVES IN CHILD DEVELOPMENT, International Universities Press, Inc., New York, 1963.
10. Romano, J.: "Basic Orientation and Education of the Medical Student," *Journal of the American Medical Association* Vol. 143, 1950, p. 409.
11. Witthower, E., and Cleghorn, R., eds.: RECENT DEVELOPMENTS IN PSYCHOMATIC MEDICINE, J. B. Lippincott Co., Philadelphia, 1957.

The developmental dimension: ✓

Concepts of health and disease in children are different from those applicable to adults, depending upon the child's capacities at a particular stage of development, the current nature of the family transactional operations, and other factors. In this section, certain broad philosophic considerations that the Committee considers pertinent will be presented. The description of specific vicissitudes in personality development and operations will be reserved for the section dealing with the actual classification.

Considerations of behavioral or personality development call for certain definitions. In this connection the Committee has chosen to employ insofar as possible definitions currently accepted in the fields of pediatrics and child development, rather than to compound confusion by introducing numerous new definitions. Thus the term *growth* is reserved for any reference to increase in physical size—whether of the total organism or any of its dimensions, parts, or tissues—involving relatively permanent tissue changes and occurring in the child's progress toward physical maturity. *Maturation* is utilized to refer to those aspects of physical as well as psychological progression that relate to the intrinsic sequential patterning of specific steps toward maturity, appearing on a built-in timetable based on largely biological or inborn sources. The term *development* is used to designate the increasing differentiation, complexity, and ultimate integration of structure, function, or behavior. Development can thus be said to encompass the interaction of maturational patterns and of experience or learning.

There is a general curve of development for the species, with a unique curve for each individual. Within the healthy range, normal *developmental variations* may occur. Some modification of the timetable may result from the effects of physical, psychological, or social stimuli. Other precocious or retarded sequences may be considered pathological because they are inappropriate for the stage of development or are out of synchrony with other dimensions of development. The concept of *developmental deviations*—beyond the range of normal variation and independent of the effects of disease or damage—can be applied to psychological and social as well as to physical dimensions.

1. Basic Principles

In regard to personality development, certain principles can be fairly readily discerned, having some parallels with physical patterns. These include *continuity* and *consistency,* with each stage of development related to and influenced by preceding stages as the personality gradually becomes more organized and consistent in its patterns of response. The *individuality* of these patterns is maintained, however, despite the tendency of certain common clusters of personality traits to emerge in older childhood and adult life. Personality development tends in general to follow a certain *sequence;* nevertheless, the rate of development, while often showing consistency, may vary considerably from individual to individual and from stage to stage within individuals. *Phases of development* can be identified. Transitional periods occur between these phases and involve *developmental crises* that must be resolved before the child can move forward to the next phase.

Although *gradual progression* is the rule, with a tendency toward the crystallization of an inner psychic structure, development is ordinarily uneven in childhood. Spurts, plateaus, and lags are characteristic, as in physical growth. Noxious stimuli of various sorts can induce temporary behavioral *regression* to more safely established levels of adaptation, or they may result in arrest or *fixation* in different dimensions of psychological development. Either intrinsic or experiential factors can produce a *developmental lag,* a serious *retardation,* or a blunting or *distortion* in one or another aspect of personality development.

Some interrelationship appears to exist among the several aspects of personality development. These embrace *intellectual, emotional, physical and social dimensions,* in all their capacities and potentialities, and relate to the psychological, physiological, and social levels previously discussed. *Parallel progress* may occur among dimensions; widely *divergent paths* may be followed, however, and much unevenness may appear. One can say that a basic ground plan of personality development exists for the individual child. Within this overall framework, founded on maturational underpinnings, each part or function is seen as having its own special time of ascendancy, based on previous steps and responding to a particular configuration of environmental stimuli. Some parallel exists with the epigenetic considerations in embryological development, for example, the effect of German measles during early pregnancy on the embryo. The basic progression appears to move from global and undifferentiated responses in early infancy toward increasing *differentiation of function* within the different dimensions. Ultimate *integration* of differentiated functional parts of the personality appears to take place in the constant interplay between the developing organism and its environment, resulting in a functioning whole that is more than the sum of its parts.

2. Maturity and the Healthy Personality

A challenging definition pertinent to development is that involved in the concept of maturity. Physical maturity, representing the point of completion of growth and the readiness for reproduction, is fairly easy to delineate, even though its time of attainment may vary considerably for individuals within the healthy range. Concepts of psychosexual and psychosocial or emotional maturity remain more difficult to define. To some extent personality development continues, or should continue, throughout the life of the individual. Unlike the physical components of the human organism, psychological and social attributes need not cease to develop when physical maturity is reached; within limits, they need not degenerate seriously with advancing age.

From the perspective presented, psychological maturity, broadly characterized, represents the point at which fundamental developmental tasks are solved, the personality structure is fully consolidated, and the individual is capable of independent and effective functioning. Of course the actual definition of the attributes of the psychologically mature or healthy individual may vary from culture to culture and from point to point in historical time. This relativity of definitions of maturity has important implications for the classification of deviations in personality functioning. Although *adaptation* and *adjustment* (the comfortable fit of the individual into a particular set of social circumstances) are attributes of the healthy personality, they are not necessarily synonymous with maturity.

The Committee agreed with the definition of the mature and healthy person as one who actively, flexibly, and rationally masters his environment most of the time; shows a unity and integrity of personality; is able to perceive the world and himself, including his own feelings, in essentially correct proportions; can postpone immediate gratifications in favor of more long-term goals; exhibits the capacities for love, work, and play; enjoys a certain sense of mental well-being; and possesses a set of values which permit him to organize his life and work while also tolerating the values of others. The truly mature individual may at times forsake adjustment and conformity for the less certain and more painful, but ultimately more rewarding and constructive, experience of attempting to alter or influence his world in a creative fashion. He also possesses the capacity for further personality development throughout adult life.

3. Developmental Stages

In the material to follow, the stages of development on the way to maturity will be designated as: (1) *infancy,* covering the period from birth to two years of age; (2) *preschool period,* or early childhood, ranging from two through five years of age; (3) *school-age period,* or later childhood, from six years until the onset of puberty (approximately 11-13 years of age in girls and 13-15 years in boys), and including the prepubertal phase; (4) *adolescence,* from the onset of puberty until the completion of biologic maturity, with early, middle, and late phases. Such stages have an arbitrary quality. They do not correspond exactly with psychosexual and psychosocial stages of development, particularly as regards the achievement of psychological maturity. Nevertheless, they represent the current coin of the realm, in that professional persons from a variety of fields can utilize them meaningfully. In addition, there is sufficient correspondence with psychological aspects of development to render them helpful at least as points of reference.

4. Constitutional Influences

The Committee felt it important to agree upon a definition of the term *constitution.* In the modern view, constitution is a process—not a given constant—and as such represents a dynamic, not a static, state. Constitutional characteristics can be said to include the sum total of the structural and functional qualities or potentialities of the individual, interacting with his physical environment and his different levels and varieties of experience, beginning with the intrauterine environment. Rather than supporting a nature versus nurture point of view, this conceptual approach to constitution assumes that hereditary endowment is modified by experiential factors throughout development to produce the individual's basic physique, his intellectual capacity, his immune response patterns, and possibly certain temperamental qualities, biological rhythms, and the capacity to tolerate tensions. The concepts of genotype and phenotype are pertinent to this view, which is in harmony with the ideas about maturation and development put forth earlier.

5. Vulnerabilities and Strengths

In his developmental march toward maturity, the child appears to undergo certain *critical phases,* during which greater vulnerability to stimuli of stressful nature may exist. As an example on the physiological level, a heightened susceptibility may be noted to particular infections, such as otitis media in preschool children or tuberculosis in adolescent girls. From a psychological perspective, infants in the second half of the first year are seen to be especially affected by significant and prolonged lack of mothering. Recent work with both human infants and animals suggests that particular patterns of social behavior in older infants and young children require for their evocation that certain stimuli occur in a particular configurational context, during appropriate or optimal developmental phases. If these stimuli are not forthcoming from a caretaking figure, serious blunting of these patterns may occur, leading at times to apparently irreversible defects in intellectual or other dimensions of development. The late preschool phase, dealing with the issues of social integration and sexual differentiation, can be considered another critical phase, as can that of adolescence, involving the need for resolution of a satisfying self-concept and the emergence of full independence.

The child in certain early developmental phases may tolerate particular stresses more readily than during later ones. The capacity of the fetus to withstand hypoxia during delivery and the immediate postnatal period is one example. Another is the power of cerebral and psychological compensation available to the young child in the event of an insult to the central nervous system. A further instance is the child's too-little-mentioned ability to cope effectively with potentially traumatic experiences. The inborn impetus toward growth and maturation characteristic of the human organism seems to provide the child with remarkable resiliency and recuperative powers even in relation to markedly stressful experiences. This appears to be true of psychological as well as physical parameters of development, thus supporting a generally optimistic view of the developmental process despite its recognized dangers.

6. Developmental Patterns

In the first several months of life, prior to the development of true object relations with a parent figure, the infant apparently has a limited capacity to screen out or to monitor stimuli from without or within. At this stage he appears to respond in an immediate and global fashion to overstimulation or to a lack of gratification of his needs ranging from nutritional to stimulus hunger, with a number of organ systems diffusely involved in the particular response.

As object relations and primitive ego functions develop, the older infant or young preschool child is able to react in a more differentiated fashion to emotional conflicts. These take place originally between himself and his environment, represented initially by the parents, and occur in the context of the young child's struggle to master himself and his environment. Such reactions at this stage are often transient and reversible, generally responding to the resolution of conflict involved in environmental shifts or supportive influences from the parents.

The further development of the mental apparatus in the late preschool and early school-age child, including the formation of the conscience or superego, together with the appearance of more effective repression of affects and of other ego mechanisms, makes it possible for him unconsciously to internalize emotional conflicts of the nature described, when these remain unresolved. At times of developmental crisis involving conflict situations the child at this level may be able to resolve the conflict and move forward to a higher level of adaptation and personality development. Or he may be unable to accomplish such a successful resolution, depending upon his adaptive capacity and the current family situation, so that repression and internalization of the conflicting emotions may take place. Conflict may thus become self-perpetuating in nature, leading to repetitive and often maladaptive attempts by the child to employ various inappropriate defensive or coping maneuvers. Thus unconscious conflict, together with the associated defenses, may become an integral part of the personality structure. The potentiality for future modification may be limited under such circumstances; this represents the model of neurosis. Or there may be a different outcome—perhaps a temporary retrogression, more long-term arrest or fixation in function or development, or decompensation and adaptive breakdown, the last-named leading to more serious psychopathological pictures characteristic of this stage of development.

In adolescence, the positive resolution of identity conflicts and role operations in relation to self, parents, and peer group may make possible the reworking of earlier developmental crises or problems. Although the vulnerability of this critical phase may permit sweeping regressions in adaptive behavior or more serious adaptive breakdown, the impetus toward development makes the prognosis for constructive realignment of the adaptive equilibrium more favorable in many adolescents than in adults.

7. *Special Considerations*

While up to this point the potentially pathologic results of anxiety and conflict have been emphasized purposefully, the possibility should not be overlooked that at certain points milder degrees of anxiety and conflict may exert a positive influence upon the child, may serve as a spur to progression and to the evolution of new and more mature coping mechanisms, promoting adaptation, individuation, mastery, and creativity. Thus the balance of progressive and regressive forces involved in development may be affected positively or negatively by anxiety and conflict, depending upon the degree of intensity, the child's developmental capacities, the responses of important persons, and other factors.

Cognitive and intellectual parameters of development have been but briefly mentioned. Space does not permit full discussion of the prevalent theories of learning and motivation in which such concepts as reinforcement (positive and negative) and reward are involved. Suffice it to say that these concepts, among them the developmental stages in cognitive operations, can enrich our understanding and are not incompatible with the views expressed, even though additional motivational factors are assumed.

8. Theoretical Assumptions

In this conceptual approach, the Committee has drawn most heavily upon psychoanalytic theory involving structural, dynamic, genetic, and adaptive aspects of the functioning of the mental apparatus. Indeed, the concepts of emotional conflict, conscious and unconscious levels of thought and feeling, the phenomenon of repression and the operation of other psychological defense mechanisms in response to anxiety, and the importance of object relations, with their vicissitudes, have become cardinal features of modern dynamic psychology and psychiatric practice. In more recent years there has been an emphasis by workers in the psychoanalytic field upon ego psychology. These workers have elaborated on earlier concepts of ego functioning, stressing the importance of such aspects as perception, discrimination, integration, thought, affect, motility, tension regulation, speech, individuation, self-perception, and reality testing. These ego functions appear to subserve coping mechanisms directed toward the solution of psychosocial tasks in development along with the additional influences of family, peer group, social class, ethnic, and other sociocultural and historical forces.

Although the Committee has found most helpful this body of theory, much of which remains to be tested systematically, there have been many other influences on its thinking. These influences derive from the fields of learning theory, neurophysiology, child development, social science, and ethology—all of which have made important contributions of their own and have significantly affected the ego-psychological emphasis. The central view employed, with these contributions from other sources, represents a set of operational constructs that appear to the Committee to describe or explain most consistently (with important exceptions) processes of personality formation and functioning in line with the psychosomatic, developmental, and psychosocial propositions. In the total conceptual framework employed, the Committee tried to incorporate useful concepts from these other fields without losing a central core of consistency and coherence.

In its broadest sense, the point of view expressed herein underlines the importance of the interaction between innate and experiential factors in the child's development as his burgeoning mental apparatus integrates external environmental forces with intrapsychic perceptions and adaptive operations. As Anna Freud[16] has pointed out in her "developmental profile," defensive or adaptive maneuvers utilized by the child will depend upon his inherent characteristics and upon his developmental level, with its available capacities. The attitudes of the parents or other persons in the social milieu will support or interfere with the use of particular mechanisms. The *balance of internal and external forces* is thus a vital factor in diagnosis and classification, as well as in the determination of modern treatment planning for child and family.

In the proposed classification, specific recommendations will be spelled out regarding diagnoses at different levels of development, with criteria indicated for each category.

Selected References

1. Allport, G. W.: PATTERN AND GROWTH IN PERSONALITY, Holt, Rinehart & Winston, Inc., New York, 1961.
2. Ausubel, D. P.: THEORY AND PROBLEMS OF EGO DEVELOPMENT, Grune & Stratton, Inc., New York, 1958.
3. Bayley, N.: "Normal Growth and Development," in P. Hoch

and J. Zubin, eds., PSYCHOPATHOLOGY OF CHILDHOOD, Grune & Stratton, Inc., New York, 1955.

4. Benedek, T.: "Parenthood as a Developmental Phase," *Journal of the American Psychoanalytic Association* Vol. 7, 1959, p. 389.

5. ————: "The Psychosomatic Implications of the Primary Unit: Mother-Child," *American Journal of Orthopsychiatry*, Vol. 19, 1949, p. 642.

6. Benjamin, J.: "Prediction and Psychopathologic Theory," in L. Jessner and E. Pavenstedt, eds., DYNAMIC PSYCHOPATHOLOGY IN CHILDHOOD, Grune & Stratton, Inc., New York, 1959.

7. Bibring, G. L.: "Some Considerations of the Psychological Processes in Pregnancy," in THE PSYCHOANALYTIC STUDY OF THE CHILD, Vol. XIV, International Universities Press, Inc., New York, 1959.

8. Bowlby, J.: "The Nature of the Child's Tie to His Mother," *International Journal of Psycho-Analysis* Vol. 39, 1958, p. 350.

9. Carmichael, L., ed.: MANUAL OF CHILD PSYCHOLOGY, John Wiley & Sons, Inc., New York, 1954.

10. Chess, S.; Thomas, A.; Birch, H. G.; and Hertzig, M.: "A Longitudinal Study of Primary Reaction Patterns in Children," *Comprehensive Psychiatry* Vol. 1, 1960, p. 103.

11. Coghill, G. E.: ANATOMY AND THE PROBLEM OF BEHAVIOR, The Macmillan Co., Inc., New York, 1929.

12. Dennis, W., ed.: READINGS IN CHILD PSYCHOLOGY, Prentice-Hall, Inc., New York, 1951.

13. Engel, G.: PSYCHOLOGICAL DEVELOPMENT IN HEALTH AND DISEASE, W. B. Saunders Co., Philadelphia, 1962.

14. Erikson, E. H.: "Growth and Crises of the Healthy Personality," in IDENTITY AND THE LIFE CYCLE, Psychological Issues, Monograph Series No. 1, International Universities Press, Inc., New York, 1959.

15. Escalona, S., and Heider, G. M.: PREDICTION AND OUTCOME: A STUDY IN CHILD DEVELOPMENT, Basic Books, Inc., New York, 1959.

16. Freud, A.: NORMALITY AND PATHOLOGY: ASSESSMENT OF DEVELOPMENT, International Universities Press, Inc., New York, 1965.

17. Freud, S.: AN OUTLINE OF PSYCHOANALYSIS, W. W. Norton & Co., Inc., New York, 1949.
18. Gesell, A., and Amatruda, C. S.: DEVELOPMENTAL DIAGNOSIS, Paul B. Hoeber, Inc., New York, 1941.
19. Hall, C. S., and Lindsey, G.: THEORIES OF PERSONALITY, John Wiley & Sons, Inc., New York, 1957.
20. Hartmann, H.: EGO PSYCHOLOGY AND THE PROBLEM OF ADAPTATION, International Universities Press, Inc., New York, 1958.
21. Hebb, D. O.: THE ORGANIZATION OF BEHAVIOR, John Wiley & Sons, Inc., New York, 1949.
22. Hooker, D.: "Reflex Activities in the Human Fetus," in R. Barker, J. Konnin, and H. Wright, eds., CHILD BEHAVIOR AND DEVELOPMENT, McGraw-Hill Book Co., Inc., New York, 1943.
23. Inhelder, B., and Piaget, J.: THE GROWTH OF LOGICAL THINKING FROM CHILDHOOD TO ADOLESCENCE, Basic Books, Inc., New York, 1958.
24. Isaacs, S.: SOCIAL DEVELOPMENT OF YOUNG CHILDREN. A STUDY OF BEGINNNINGS, Harcourt Brace, New York, 1933.
25. Jahoda, M.: CURRENT CONCEPTS OF POSITIVE MENTAL HEALTH, Basic Books, Inc., New York, 1960.
26. Josselyn, I.: PSYCHOSOCIAL DEVELOPMENT OF CHILDREN, Family Service Association of America, New York, 1948.
27. Lewin, K.: "Behavior and Development as a Function of the Total Situation," in L. Carmichael, ed., MANUAL OF CHILD PSYCHOLOGY, John Wiley & Sons, Inc., New York, 1954.
28. Lorenz, K.: KING SOLOMON'S RING, Thomas Y. Crowell Co., New York, 1952.
29. Luria, A. R.: THE ROLE OF SPEECH IN THE REGULATION OF NORMAL AND ABNORMAL BEHAVIOR, Pergamon Press, Ltd., London, 1961.
30. McClearn, G. E.: "Genetics and Behavior Development," in M. and L. Hoffman, eds., REVIEW OF CHILD DEVELOPMENT RESEARCH, Russell Sage Foundation, New York, 1964.
31. McGraw, M. B.: THE NEUROMUSCULAR MATURATION OF THE HUMAN INFANT, Columbia University Press, New York, 1952.
32. Montagu, M. F. A.: "Constitutional and Prenatal Factors in Infant and Child Health," in M. J. E. Senn, ed., SYMPOSIUM ON

THE HEALTHY PERSONALITY, Josiah Macy, Jr. Foundation, New York, 1950.

33. Mowrer, O. H.: LEARNING THEORY AND PERSONALITY DYNAMICS: SELECTED PAPERS, The Ronald Press Co., Inc., New York, 1950.

34. Murphy, L. B.: THE WIDENING WORLD OF CHILDHOOD: PATHS TOWARD MASTERY, Basic Books, Inc., New York, 1962.

35. Richmond, J. B., and Lipton, E. L.: "Some Aspects of the Neurophysiology of the Newborn and Their Implications for Child Development," in L. Jessner and E. Pavenstedt, eds., DYNAMIC PSYCHOPATHOLOGY IN CHILDHOOD, Grune & Stratton, Inc., New York, 1959.

36. Scott, J. P.: "Critical Periods in Behavioral Development," Science, Vol. 138, 1962, p. 949.

37. Shakow, D., and Rapaport, D.: THE INFLUENCE OF FREUD ON AMERICAN PSYCHOLOGY, Psychological Issues, Monograph Series No. 13, International Universities Press, Inc., New York, 1964.

38. Sontag, L. W.; Baker, C. T.; and Nelson, V. L.: MENTAL GROWTH AND PERSONALITY DEVELOPMENT: A LONGITUDINAL STUDY, Society for Research in Child Development, Series No. 68, Monograph 23, No. 2, Purdue University Press, Lafayette, Indiana, 1958.

39. Spitz, R.: A GENETIC FIELD THEORY OF EGO FORMATION, International Universities Press, Inc., New York, 1959.

40. Stendler, C. B.: "Critical Periods in Socialization and Overdependency," Child Development, Vol. 23, 1952, p. 3.

41. Witmer, H. L., and Kotinsky, R., eds.: PERSONALITY IN THE MAKING, Harper & Brothers, Inc., New York, 1952.

Psychosocial considerations:

The child's personality development, with its strengths and its vicissitudes, is assumed to be influenced by multiple etiologic or shaping forces. These may arise from or take place at any one of the three basic levels of organization, with reverberations "up" or "down" the intercommunicating open systems. The final outcome may be difficult to predict until psychological maturity is reached, since there may be later resolution of earlier problems, depending upon the balance of external and internal forces. Accordingly the Committee feels that no absolute position could or should be taken, at this stage of knowledge, regarding the exclusive or overriding importance of any one set of etiologic factors, whether of an inborn or an experiential nature. Both sets of forces are undoubtedly involved, with varying degrees of emphasis, in all disturbances in development or adaptation.

Regardless of the relative weighting of influential variables, the effect of environmental experience upon the child is certainly of vital significance. Its impact appears to be more intense in the earlier phases of development because of the great dependency of human young upon caretaking figures. These areas of impact and influence will be discussed in some detail.

1. Parent-Child Relationships

The child's psychosocial milieu is at first the family; his earliest and most influential experiences take place in the context of parent-child relationships, operating within the transactional field of the networks of family interpersonal contacts. Despite our recognition of the importance of these relationships and their vicissitudes for the developing child, our knowledge of the ingredients which make up healthy parent-child interactions is still limited. Truly systematic clinical research instruments for the accurate delineation and measurement of such interactions have only begun to be developed. In addition, the available data have been interpreted from differing conceptual points of view. Among several possible theoretical systems dealing with this area, the Committee has felt that Erikson's[10] concepts are especially pertinent. These refer to the need for the solution by the child of *psychosocial tasks in development* at differing stages in parent-child, family, and societal contexts. He conceives of psychosocial conflicts that are characteristic of each period. He further postulates that the child, with the help of the parents and later figures within his expanding social radius, must resolve the conflict at each stage, thus passing through a developmental crisis and moving forward to the next stage.

Psychosocial tasks of this type include the need to establish a sense of trust and to master the conflicting sense of mistrust in the infant up to one year of age; a sense of autonomy versus a sense of shame or doubt in the toddler; a sense of initiative versus guilt in the late preschool phase; a sense of industry versus inferiority in later childhood; and a sense of identity versus identity diffusion in the adolescent. This approach, as set forth by Erikson, underlines the central role of the parents, with the growing help of siblings, peer group, teachers and other adult models, in the gradual solution of the child's psychosocial tasks; such psychosocial phases correlate in broad measure with psychosexual and intrapsychic aspects of development, as well as with intellectual and physical dimensions. Erikson further regards personality development as continuing throughout adult life. This view lends support to the idea that a "fit" is needed between continued parental solutions of later psychosocial tasks and the child's developing psychosocial needs. If such a fit is not achieved, a developmental push or drag upon the child may result, deriving from the parents' unresolved needs and related in part to their own earlier experiences.

These concepts are in harmony with those developed by others who see the parent-child relationship not as a back-and-forth interaction but as a transactional operation or a mutually reciprocal interactional system, the characteristics of each simultaneously influencing the other. Although the handling of the child by the parents is vitally important, especially in the early stages, the child's behavioral and developmental characteristics, beginning with his first feeding response, may affect the parent as feedback operations, often setting up a "circus" movement. Thus the nature of the relationship between child and parent is at least partially determined by the child's contributions to the mutually reciprocal and reverberating parent-child unit or system. The individual personality characteristics of the parents, the quality of their previous experience, their conscious and unconscious attitudes toward child-rearing and the particular child, the influence of intercurrent events during the pregnancy and neonatal period, their abilities to work together harmoniously as parents and as husband and wife, and their capacities to perceive and respond to the needs of the child as a developing individual rather than primarily in terms of their own vicarious needs are all important ingredients. These and other variables from the parents' side interact with the child's physical and behavioral characteristics, with his unfolding genic potentialities and maturational patterns, and with various fortuitous events, such as illness or accident; in so doing they determine the quality of the parent-child relationship, as well as the nature of its contribution to the child's current adaptive capacity, his state of health or disease, and his long-term personality development.

To return to the necessity for a fit between the parents' developing psychosocial equipment and that of the child: In this context, the parent must also adapt to certain inherent rhythms and reaction patterns in the child, in terms of his activity level, threshholds of response to differing types of stimuli, and other similar variables. Different parents may respond differently to different children or to the same child at differing levels of development, depending upon the parent's own characteristics or needs. In like measure, the child must also make some adaptation to the parents' characteristics, rhythms of work, activity, sleep, and the like. The resiliency of most children enables them to make these adaptations, although some children do not adapt successfully. The wise clinician recognizes that the parent as well as the child has needs and that parents do change and develop in their parenting capacities.

Concepts such as those presented above support the notion that, although the child's early relationships and experiences are importantly formative, they are not necessarily permanent and unchangeable in their influence upon his personality development. Psychosocial tasks not completed at earlier levels may be resolved at later stages, depending upon the child's inherent capacities, his later experiences, and the course of *parent development* and family evolution. Within such limits and in the light of the mass of clinical evidence and research data which has been accumulated in recent years, the importance of adequate parenting for the child's healthy personality development, from physical, psychological, or social points of view, today cannot be questioned.

Pathogenic Factors:

Among other variables, actual, threatened, or symbolic disruptions in parent-child relationships have been implicated in a wide range of childhood disorders of adaptation or development. These range from predominantly psychological disorders, such as depression, environmental retardation in psychomotor development, psychoneuroses, so-called functional psychoses, and antisocial personality disorders, through illnesses in which psychological and physiological disturbances may coexist, as in hospitalism, ulcerative colitis, and marasmus or failure to thrive, to certain emotional components of behavior disturbances associated with structural changes in the central nervous system.

Despite considerable knowledge of this nature, our understanding of the precise character and degree of influence upon personality development of faulty parent-child relationships remains somewhat limited today. The deleterious effects of sweeping emotional deprivation or understimulation (occurring overtly in broken families or covertly in intact families) and of marked overprotection, overcontrol, overpermissiveness, overindulgence, inconsistency, or overstimulation, and, more rarely, of open rejection or neglect, occasionally involving willful injury or inadequate feeding, are well documented. Disturbances may take place in particular dimensions of parent-child relationships, involving insufficiency, distortion, and discontinuity of relatedness between parent and child, as well as in other dimensions related to control, acceptance, or other variables.

Although specific, relatively pathogenic child-rearing *techniques* ranging from overpunitive to overpermissive behavior can be identified in broad outline, evidence is accumulating to support the view that unhealthy parental *attitudes,* often unconscious, may be more significant in their crippling effects upon the child's personality development than any single child-rearing technique or its specific timing or dosage. Clusters of child-rearing techniques may be associated with certain unhealthy parental attitudes, and a number of disturbing events in the parent-child relationship occurring over time, rather than any one emotionally traumatic experience, seem ordinarily to be involved in the outcome.

Gross disturbances in these dimensions do seem to have pathogenic effects upon the child. The results of more subtle disturbances in the parent-child relationship are still difficult to gauge. At the present time, considerable "postdiction" but limited prediction can be accomplished in relation to these and other dimensions. Antecedent variables of physical or psychosocial nature must be taken into account in assessing the personality outcome, as must later events and developmental steps which may modify the result.

As a result of all these considerations, the Committee has felt that no classification can as yet be made of childhood psychological disorders in relation to specific pathogenic characteristics of the parent-child relationship. Recent work dealing with certain identifiable patterns of personality operation in parents of psychotic and neurotic children and with the superego lacunae demonstrated in the parents of some delinquent children supports the ultimate likelihood of discovering some specificity in parent-child relationships for certain disorders. In addition, other workers have cogently conceptualized the differential reactivation of past areas of conflict in the parent or parents as related to the developmental stage and characteristics of the child, and have noted the production of localized neurotic conflict between parent and child as one of several patterns of interaction and of "contagious" transmission of symptoms. Such advances in understanding of parent-child transactions are greatly helpful, suggesting some more focused methods of therapy. However, they leave us far from the classificatory stage.

2. Family Interactions

Current understanding of family interrelationships fits comfortably within the conceptual approach outlined. Such knowledge, within the limits available, is summarized fully in the report, INTEGRATION AND CONFLICT IN FAMILY BEHAVIOR,[15] by the Committee on the Family of the Group for the Advancement of Psychiatry, and in other publications by workers in the field. Within the family the transactional equilibrium between parent and child must be extended to other members in regard to their mutual interactions with each other in varying combinations —from diadic, triangular, or other subgroups to the transactional operations of the total family as a unit or a small group of persons. The degree of intactness and cohesiveness of the family, its overall patterns of communication, leadership and role functions, its value orientations, and the nature and extent of its integration into the external community, in addition to the subgroup operations among its individual members, appear to be involved in the maintenance of a *family adaptive equilibrium,* or a balance of familial interpersonal forces.

Significant disruptions in this equilibrium may affect parent-child relationships and, indirectly, the adaptive capacity of the particular child, thus acting as a stressful stimulus at the social level of organization; reverberations may occur at psychological or physiological levels or at both. The altered behavior of the child may then serve as a feedback mechanism to affect unfavorably one or both parents or to call out preferential behavior on the part of one parent toward a sibling.

A variety of crises may arise in family operations, ranging from the illness of a child to the death of a family member. In the healthy family unit, such crises may temporarily alter patterns of communication, interpersonal transaction, and role functioning. However, the flexibility and cohesiveness of the family unit is not lost. A new and different equilibrium can be established, sometimes at a higher, more effectively adaptive level, permitting the concept of *family development.* In a less healthy family system, significant conflicts may occur among its members and disequilibrium may ensue. This disequilibrium may be dealt with at the cost of the psychological health of one individual—for example, a child who may unconsciously be made a scapegoat for family tensions. Actual family breakdown or disintegration may of course arise from death, divorce, or other sources, with frequent though not invariable pathological repercussions for the personality development of children at vulnerable levels.

Other observations on pathological family situations include the effect, over several generations, of individual family members with serious psychopathological disorders, who may act as "carriers" of disturbed behavior. Deeply pathological and precariously poised equilibria in families with seriously disturbed members may be based on unhealthy relationships of intensely complementary, interlocking or dovetailing nature (pseudomutual, double bind) between parent and child, parent and parent, or other subgroup combinations. The death, illness, departure for college, or even improvement during psychological treatment of one of such deeply interdependent partners may lead to the decompensation and illness of the other, with marked depression or even psychosis.

Further reports dealing with these and other aspects of family functioning suggest other characteristic patterns related to particular types of pathological development in child members. Such a pattern may be found in certain types of delinquent behavior, which occur frequently in families with little cohesiveness and with defects in disciplinary patterns; or in the relatively specific conflictual family patterns or subpatterns operative in the clinical pictures of schizophrenia, other types of psychosis, psychoneuroses, and certain psychophysiologic disorders.

As with parent-child relationships, the Committee feels that such suggestive evidence for specific correlations between family patterns and individual child disorders is not yet sufficient to warrant attempts at etiologic classification. The differences in conceptual framework employed by a number of workers in attempting the difficult task of evolving a model of family behavior are pertinent. For purposes of diagnostic formulation, however, it is important to consider the various forms of family operations presently known—from the healthy family response in a crisis situation to the noncohesive, multiproblem family. Furthermore, the therapeutic approach is influenced by such a formulation, drawing also on individual personality pictures of child and parent, parent-child interactions and other variables.

3. Sociocultural Influences

In addition to the transactions within the social field of the family unit, other phenomena, involving social interaction within the larger fields of the community, state, and national society, must be taken into account in considering the response of the individual to significantly stressful stimuli at the social or interpersonal level. Variations in family structure, mores, and functioning, as well as in child-rearing techniques, occur from one ethnic group to another and from urban to rural communities. Historical and sociological trends are also pertinent. One example may be seen in the shift to the two-generation, highly mobile family unit, reaching toward the middle-class model and away from the extended-kinship family, occurring within the trends toward industrialization and urbanization of the past century.

The incidence of mental illness, particularly psychosis, seems to be related to social class and associated factors in a fashion still poorly understood. Shifts in symptoms may apparently occur in movements of ethnic groups, during transition from lower- to middle-class socioeconomic status or over historical epochs.

Although these factors, which are not yet fully confirmed, are certainly of importance, their relevance for the purpose of classification is not yet clear. They can help to explain certain types of behavior in particular segments of our society, however, and may play a contributory role in many types of illness. Variations in the definition and degree of tolerance (or even encouragement) of symptomatic or "sick" behavior, according to the particular subcultural group, are pertinent to clinical work, as are the differing attitudes among families from varying backgrounds toward illness and the roles of patient and doctor. Awareness of such factors can help physicians and other professional workers avoid culture-bound attitudes or stereotyping groups on the basis of social class, which, in turn, may affect the nature of the treatment or other services offered.

Selected References

1. Ackerman, N. W.: THE PSYCHODYNAMICS OF FAMILY LIFE, Basic Books, Inc., New York, 1958.
2. Allen, F. A.: "Mother-Child Separation—Process or Event?" in EMOTIONAL PROBLEMS OF EARLY CHILDHOOD, Basic Books, Inc., New York, 1955, pp. 325-327.
3. Bakwin, H.: "Emotional Deprivation in Infants," *Journal of Pediatrics*, Vol. 35, 1949, pp. 512-521.
4. Bell, N. W., and Vogel, E. F., eds.: THE FAMILY, Free Press of Glencoe, Ill., 1960.
5. Bowlby, J.: MATERNAL CARE AND MENTAL HEALTH Monograph Series No. 2. World Health Organization, Geneva, 1951.
6. Brody, S.: PATTERNS OF MOTHERING, International Universities Press, Inc., New York, 1956.
7. Caldwell, B. M.: "The Effects of Infant Care," in M. Hoffman, ed., REVIEW OF CHILD DEVELOPMENT RESEARCH, Vol. I, Russell Sage Foundation, New York, 1964.
8. Caplan, G., ed.: PREVENTION OF MENTAL DISORDERS IN CHILDREN, Basic Books, Inc., New York, 1961.
9. DEPRIVATION OF MATERNAL CARE: A REASSESSMENT OF ITS EFFECTS, Public Health Papers, No. 14, World Health Organization, Geneva, 1962.
10. Erikson, E. H.: CHILDHOOD AND SOCIETY, 2nd ed., W. W. Norton & Co. Inc., New York, 1963.
11. Finzer, W. F., and Kisley, A. J.: "Localized Neurotic Interaction," *Journal of the American Academy of Child Psychiatry*, Vol. 3, 1964, p. 265.
12. Fisher, S., and Mendell, D.: "The Communication of Neurotic Patterns over Two and Three Generations," in N. Bell and E. Vogel, eds., THE FAMILY, Free Press of Glencoe, Ill., 1960.
13. Friend, M. R.: "The Historical Development of Family Diagnosis," *Social Service Review*, Vol. 34, 1960, pp. 2-16.
14. Fries, M. E.: "Psychosomatic Relationships between Mother and Infant," *Psychosomatic Medicine*, Vol. 6, 1944, pp. 159-162.
15. GAP (Group for the Advancement of Psychiatry) Committee on the Family: INTEGRATION AND CONFLICT IN FAMILY BEHAVIOR, GAP Report No. 27, New York, August, 1954.

16. Garmezy, N.: Clarke, A. R.; and Stockner, C.: "Child Rearing Attitudes of Mothers and Fathers as Reported by Schizophrenic and Normal Parents," *Journal of Abnormal and Social Psychology*, Vol. 63, 1961, p. 178.

17. Glazer, K., and Eisenberg, L.: "Maternal Deprivation," *Pediatrics*, Vol. 18, 1956, p. 626.

18. Glueck, S., and Glueck, E.: PREDICTING DELINQUENCY AND CRIME, Harvard University Press, Cambridge, Mass. 1959.

19. Goldfarb, W.: "Emotional and Intellectual Consequences of Psychologic Deprivation in Infancy: A Reevaluation," in P. Hoch and J. Zubin, eds., PSYCHOPATHOLOGY OF CHILDHOOD, Grune & Stratton, Inc., New York, 1955.

20. Halliday, J. L.: PSYCHOSOCIAL MEDICINE: A STUDY OF THE SICK SOCIETY, W. W. Norton & Co., Inc., New York, 1948.

21. Harlow, H. F., and Zimmerman, R. R.: "Affectional Responses in the Infant Monkey," *Science*, Vol. 130, 1959, p. 421.

22. Hollingshead, A. B., and Redlich, F. C.: SOCIAL CLASS AND MENTAL ILLNESS: A COMMUNITY STUDY, John Wiley & Sons, Inc., New York, 1958.

23. Jackson, D. D., and Weakland, J. H.: SCHIZOPHRENIC SYMPTOMS AND FAMILY INTERACTION, *Archives of Genetic Psychiatry*, Vol. 1, 1959, p. 618.

24. Johnson, A. M.: "Sanctions for Superego Lacunae of Adolescence," in K. R. Eissler, ed., SEARCHLIGHTS ON DELINQUENCY, International Universities Press, Inc., New York, 1949.

25. Kaplan, D. M.: "A Concept of Acute Situational Disorders," *Social Work*, Vol. 7, 1962, p. 15.

26. Kaufman, I.; Frank, T.; Heins, L.; Herrick, J.; Reiser, D.; and Willer, L.: "Treatment Implications of a New Classification of Parents of Schizophrenic Children," *American Journal of Psychiatry*, Vol. 116, 1960, p. 932.

27. Levy, D. M.: "Primary Affect Hunger," *American Journal of Psychiatry*, Vol. 94, 1937, p. 643.

28. Lidz, T.; Cornelison, A.; Fleck, S.; and Terry, D.: "The Intrafamilial Environment of the Schizophrenic Patient. IV. Parental Personalities and Family Interaction," *American Journal of Orthopsychiatry*, Vol. 28, 1951, p. 764.

29. Lindemann, E.: "The Psychosocial Position on Etiology," in

H. D. Kruse, ed., INTEGRATING THE APPROACHES TO MENTAL DISEASE, Hoeber-Harper, Inc., New York, 1957.

30. Maas, H. S., and Engler, R. E.: CHILDREN IN NEED OF PARENTS, Columbia University Press, New York, 1959.

31. Mead, M., and Wolfenstein, M.: CHILDHOOD IN CONTEMPORARY CULTURES, University of Chicago Press, Chicago, 1955.

32. Miller, N. E., and Dollard, J.: SOCIAL LEARNING AND IMITATION, Yale University Press, New Haven, Conn., 1941.

33.(a) Opler, M. K., ed.: CULTURE AND MENTAL HEALTH, The Macmillan Co., Inc., New York, 1959.

33.(b) Orlansky, H.: "Infant Care and Personality," *Psychological Bulletin*, Vol. 46, 1949, p. 1.

34. Parsons, T.: "Social Structure and the Development of Personality: Freud's Contributions to the Integration of Psychology and Sociology," *Psychiatry*, Vol. 21, 1958, pp. 321-322.

35. Pollak, O.: "A Family Diagnosis Model," *Social Service Review*, Vol. 34, 1960, pp. 19-28.

36. Rank, B.; Putnam, M.; and Rochlin, G.: "The Significance of Emotional Climate in Early Feeding Difficulties," *Psychosomatic Medicine*, Vol. 10, 1948, pp. 279-283.

37. Riessman, D.; Glazer, N.; and Denny, R.: THE LONELY CROWD: A STUDY OF THE CHANGING AMERICAN CHARACTER, Yale University Press, New Haven, Conn., 1950.

38. Robertson, J.: YOUNG CHILDREN IN HOSPITALS, Basic Books, Inc., New York, 1958.

39. Rose, A., ed.: MENTAL HEALTH AND MENTAL DISORDER: A SOCIOLOGICAL APPROACH, W. W. Norton & Co., Inc., New York, 1955.

40. Roudinesco, J.; David, M.; and Micolas, J.: "Responses of Young Children to Separation from Their Mothers. I. Observation of Children Ages 12 to 17 Months Recently Separated from Their Families and Living in an Institution," *Courrier* (*Centre International de l'Enfance*), Vol. 2, 1952, p. 66.

41. Ruesch, J., and Bateson, G.: COMMUNICATION: THE SOCIAL MATRIX OF SOCIETY, W. W. Norton & Co., Inc., New York, 1951.

42. Sears, R. R.; Maccoby, E. E.; and Levin, H.: PATTERNS OF CHILD REARING, Row, Peterson, Evanston, Ill., 1957.

43. Singer, M. T., and Wynne, L. C.: "Differentiating Characteristics of Parents of Childhood Schizophrenics, Childhood Neurotics, and Young Adult Schizophrenics," *American Journal of Psychiatry*, Vol. 120, 1963, p. 234.

44. Spiegel, J. P.: "The Resolution of Role Conflict within the Family," *Psychiatry*, Vol. 20, 1957, p. 1.

45. Spitz, R. A.: "Hospitalism: An Inquiry into the Genesis of Psychiatric Conditions in Early Childhood: A Follow-up Report," in PSYCHOANALYTIC STUDY OF THE CHILD, Vol. II, 1946, p. 113.

46. Sullivan, H. S.: "Introduction to the Study of Interpersonal Relations," *Psychiatry*, Vol. 1, 1938, p. 121.

47. Whiting, J. W. M., and Child, I. L.: CHILD TRAINING AND PERSONALITY: A CROSS-CULTURAL STUDY, Yale University Press, New Haven, Conn., 1953.

48. Yarrow, L. J.: "Separation from Parents during Early Childhood," in REVIEW OF CHILD DEVELOPMENT RESEARCH, Vol. I, Russell Sage Foundation, New York, 1964.

2

CONSIDERATIONS REGARDING ORGANIZATION AND USAGE OF PROPOSED CLASSIFICATION

From the foregoing conceptual framework embracing psychosomatic, developmental, and psychosocial points of view, certain considerations apply directly to the purpose of classification—the goal of the Committee's report. Other considerations, as has been suggested, apply more appropriately to the area of diagnostic formulation, the principles of which have been set forth in the Committee's publication, THE DIAGNOSTIC PROCESS IN CHILD PSYCHIATRY.* It is apparent that classification of individual personality pictures is an arbitrary process, necessary and helpful but artificial in many respects. The psychosomatic concept indicates the unity of response of the human organism, with psychological syndromes representing only one component of its participation in the response at physiological, psychological, and social levels. The developmental dimension underwrites the relativity of classification, depending upon the developmental stage and the parameter of development which is selected, together with other factors. The psychosocial proposition promotes the conclusion that the clinician must accept the family rather than the individual alone as the essential unit for the study and treatment of health and disease. All the propositions mentioned support the concept of multiple etiologic factors of predisposing, contributory, precipitating, and perpetuating nature involved in states of health or disease, as suggested by the unitary theory.

The ideal scheme of classification would, as has been implied,

---

* See the Bibliography preceding the Appendix Bibliography at the end of this book.

208

permit a synthesis of the clinical picture, the psychodynamic and psychosocial factors, "genetic" considerations regarding the level of origin, the major etiological forces, a concise prognosis, and the appropriate method of treatment. The conceptual framework described would nevertheless permit the conclusion that such a clinical-dynamic-genetic-etiological scheme of classification is presently premature if not unrealistic. From the information currently available, only the clinical-descriptive aspects can be dealt with in a classification that is susceptible to the use of statistical methods and that can be employed by people from differing schools of thought. As of today, the other components must still be left for a diagnostic formulation.

Even within a clinical-descriptive approach, what one sees and describes in the collection of data depends in part upon one's point of view. To meet this problem the Committee has attempted to set forth operational definitions of clinical categories, based upon the conceptual framework proposed, with which it is hoped clinicians from varying backgrounds can agree. Some inferences regarding etiology, prognostic outlook, and treatability are inevitably implicit in such definitions, derived from clinical experience; these definitions have been held to what is, for the Committee, an irreducible minimum. Some workers will be interested in organizing the collection of clinical data in a diagnostic formulation, on the basis of dynamic-genetic factors, parent-child relationships, family modes of transaction, and demographic or other sociocultural influences, as well as other relevant factors of etiologic significance (insofar as these are understood). A suggested frame of reference for such a diagnostic formulation is included in the Appendix herein, based upon but expanding the Committee's earlier discussion of the diagnostic process. It is hoped that the classification as offered will make possible the collection of data on a descriptive-dynamic level of a more uniform, universal, and useful nature leading to the crystallization and reformulation of scientific constructs that can ultimately permit a more ideal classification.

In spite of the limitations mentioned, the conceptual framework outlined has permitted the Committee to make certain innovations in the use of nomenclature and in the approach to classification. The category *healthy responses,* considered in relation to the stage of development in its psychosocial context, has been included for the first time in any system,* and appropriate subcategories have been defined in line with the conceptual scheme proposed. Of course only the passage of time and careful follow-up studies can support the accuracy of this diagnosis when it is made. The Committee felt that such a category was necessary in order to permit the identification of healthy patterns of response and to avoid as well the traditional tendency to magnify minor problems and fit the child into a pathological category or diagnose the absence of disease. If the clinician has available a scheme for the further classification of healthy personality patterns, this of course may be used according to the particular organizing framework, even though no such universal scheme seems as yet workable to the Committee.

Another new category in the proposed system is *developmental deviations* over and beyond the variations within the healthy range. (Cameron** and, more recently, Settlage** have suggested the importance of such a category and sketched its broad outlines.) These deviations are defined as they pertain to overall deviations in maturational rate or sequence or to different aspects of personality development. Most clinicians recognize children with such deviations but are unable to classify them under existing schemes. The precise usefulness of this category and its particular subcategories will be determined only by its employment over time. In one sense it can be construed to be extremely broad and to cover any disorder during childhood development. Nevertheless, the more specific concept upon which the category is founded seemed to the Committee vital and potentially helpful. Later change of the working diagnosis based on follow-up data may be necessary for this, as for any other category, in

---

* Chess (Ref. 5, p. 324) included the category of "normal" in her classification, while Ross (Ref. 20, p. 325) referred to "absence of emotional maldevelopment."
** See Reference 4, page 324, and Reference 22, page 325.

order to subserve initial classification and more systematic data collection which can further the understanding of the natural history of particular syndromes.

Still another new feature in the classification of childhood disorders is the detailed Symptom List available for use of the clinician. The Standard Nomenclature contains a symptom list but this is designed more appropriately for adults. The Symptom List for children as organized herein is set up to permit description and recording in greater detail of units of symptomatic behavior which may be associated with different disorders, occurring individually or in clusters, at different age levels or involving change over periods of time. For convenience of usage it is presented under a system of headings indicating different types of behavior. Certain specific symptoms may be listed, under different nosological headings, in relation to the major clinical diagnosis. Thus enuresis may be shown as an age-appropriate phenomenon in a young preschool child under the heading, *healthy response;* as a symptom of a regressive nature in a *reactive disorder;* as a continuing feature of a *developmental deviation;* as part of a neurotic picture involving *conversion mechanisms;* or as one symptom in a *chronic personality disorder* or a *psychosis.* Similarly with encopresis and other symptoms. Only in this way can data be organized systematically in relation to the evolution and shifting of symptom patterns or part reactions and their association with differing personality pictures.

In the remainder of the classification, new elements are confined to the subcategories, where they have been introduced as indicated in the definitions. In order to avoid confusion and change for the sake of change only, many important features of the Standard Nomenclature have been retained. In such instances, however, the categories have been redefined for use with children. Also, certain nomenclatural terms have been altered by the Committee with a view to greater conceptual clarity for a classification of childhood disorders.

The categories of psychoneurotic disorders, personality disorders, and psychoses have been preserved as representing clinical pictures on which agreement among clinicians can be fairly readily obtained on a descriptive level with the definitions developed for childhood. The term *transient situational personality disorder,* presently found in the Standard Nomenclature and embracing adjustment reactions, stress reactions, etc., has been replaced by the term *reactive disorder* (for which Cameron has also set a precedent). This change has been made in order to avoid the looseness in the words *adjustment* and *stress,* to distinguish this category from personality disorders of a more structured and chronic nature, and to emphasize the reaction of the child to external stimuli rather than the nature of the external stimuli themselves, with all their relative qualities. In order to deal consistently with this shift in emphasis and terminology, all other categories have been termed *disorders* rather than reactions, as they are referred to in the Standard Nomenclature, with the exception of healthy responses, developmental deviations, mental retardation, and brain syndromes. In the broad sense, all disturbances involving predominantly psychological components represent reactions or reaction types; the term *reactive* is employed herein in its narrower sense, however, in line with the conceptual approach already described. Where the reaction is primarily related to internal factors, another diagnosis, for example, that of healthy response (developmental crisis), should be made.

In the classification of psychophysiologic disorders, brain syndromes, and mental retardation, the Committee faced a dilemma. The other categories already mentioned deal in general with total personality responses, although some of the developmental deviations and the reactive disorders may involve only particular aspects. However, psychophysiologic disorders represent principally end-organ or organ system responses, even though total personality factors may be involved. Most brain syndromes and many cases of mental retardation permit current classification on the basis of specific etiologic agents of predominantly physical nature. In these, the total personality is certainly affected, but the personality patterns involved may vary considerably in childhood. To be completely consistent, some new way of classifying end-organ responses and disturbances in brain functioning should be found that would integrate these consistently into the conceptual scheme proposed. At the same time, such a step—admittedly a difficult conceptual one—would throw out established categories that involve significantly identified etiological factors, partial as these may be at times to the total picture of personality development.

In dealing with this question, the Committee felt that established categories should be retained and that multiple classificatory categories could be utilized. In line with the conceptual approach, whenever a more total personality diagnosis, such as psychoneurosis, personality disorder, reactive disorder, developmental deviation, or functional psychosis, together with any of their subcategories, is applicable to a child with chronic brain damage or mental retardation, it should be employed. A young child with brain damage may show a particular syndrome of hyperactivity, impulsivity, and distractibility but may later develop an obsessive-compulsive personality pattern, for example. Similarly, a child with mental retardation (which may in certain instances be really only one form of developmental deviation) may exhibit overly dependent or oppositional personality trends as well as a psychoneurotic or psychotic personality picture. Where the behavior of children in these two categories does not fall into any organized pattern, the Symptom List will permit recording of the symptomatic aspects of behavior, permitting later follow-up of patterns that may emerge during development or treatment. Children with psychophysiologic disorders exhibiting end-organ responses should consistently receive a personality diagnosis drawn from one of the appropriate categories.

In line with the conceptual framework, reactions to predominantly physical illness are viewed as relatively nonspecific. They would thus require a diagnosis of the type of psychological disorder in addition to the separate diagnosis of the basic physical illness. Classification of reactions to acute illness would frequently involve reactive disorders, manifested by depression or separation anxiety, with specified symptoms drawn from the Symptom

List; other disorders may of course occur, including psychotic disorders or the decompensation of a chronic personality disorder. In the case of chronic illness or handicap, the type of personality disorder or other psychopathological disorder associated with the disease picture should be specified as overly dependent, overly independent, psychotic, or other, with etiologic considerations left for the diagnostic formulation.

Special diagnostic problems—for example, those offered by hypochondriacal tendencies or by the concepts embracing borderline, so-called pseudo neurotic, incipient or prepsychotic states—are dealt with in the individual definitions. Although the handling of such diagnostic challenges may be somewhat arbitrary in certain instances, the scheme proposed offers sufficient flexibility to permit more than one way of handling them in a reasonably systematized fashion. For the handling of syndromes that may be described in the future and for the purpose of dealing with an occasional picture that may not fit the categories proposed, the major category of *Other* has been provided, with similar subcategories under each of the major and minor headings. This arrangement also permits clinicians who may not agree with the definitions offered to categorize children in their own fashion yet be able to find them easily for statistical purposes. The system proposed, including the Symptom List, can be easily programmed for computer applications because of the emphasis on descriptive operational definitions within the appropriate conceptual framework.

The problem of mixed disorders is a challenging one, from nosological and statistical points of view. For such disorders the Committee recommends that more than one clinical diagnosis be employed, as in the Standard Nomenclature, with the predominant pattern given primary listing. For example, mixed psychophysiologic and conversion disorders may occur; these require multiple diagnoses in addition to the total personality diagnosis, as well as any other symptomatic patterns drawn from the Symptom List. A reactive disorder may be superimposed upon a chronic personality disorder—a picture that also can be indicated in this fashion.

The Committee has not included eponymic disorders like the syndrome of Gilles de la Tourette or Heller's disease in the classification as such, since these are relatively rare in childhood. They can be classified under the appropriate personality category or under brain syndromes, depending upon the clinician's impressions, with the symptomatic manifestations taken from the Symptom List. The same can be done with certain syndromes such as hyperactivity, which may have either predominantly psychological or predominantly somatic sources.

Modifying statements should be added to the major categorization, as in the Standard Nomenclature. These would incorporate the dimensions of *acuteness or chronicity* (with acuteness distinguished from reversibility); *degree of severity* (mild, moderate, or severe), and the *manifest nature of individual symptoms,* drawn from the Symptom List. Although certain disorders, such as psychoneuroses, personality disorders, and particular types of psychotic disorders, are viewed in the Committee's conceptual framework as occurring only after a particular point in development which permits their appearance, the broad chronological stage and *developmental period* should be specified in each instance (infancy, early childhood, later childhood, or adolescence). This kind of approach can serve as a clinical check on the Committee's conceptualizations and clinical notions as to the incidence of differing disorders at varying developmental levels. Such a descriptive designation refers only to the child's developmental stage at the time of diagnostic study and classification; for reasons mentioned earlier, it would leave for diagnostic formulation the more complicated issue of the level at which the disorder originated.

Questions about the degree of psychiatric or social impairment, the prognostic outlook, and other matters, such as the specific developmental capacities and positive adaptive features, because of their complexity in the childhood period still require individual decisions regarding data collection procedures by the individual clinician. These are discussed, together with matters of diagnostic formulation, in the Appendix.

For the sake of clarity, several examples of the nomenclature which can be used in actual classification are presented, drawing upon principal and subcategories as well as the Symptom List.

1. *Healthy response* of early childhood—developmental crisis type, acute, mild, manifested by separation anxiety and clinging behavior.

2. *Reactive disorder* of early childhood—acute, moderate, manifested by regressive encopresis, thumb-sucking, and withdrawn behavior.

3. *Developmental deviation* of later childhood—delayed maturational pattern type, chronic, moderate, manifested by impulsive behavior, low frustration tolerance, continued enuresis, reading disability, and persistence of prelogical thought processes.

4. *Psychoneurotic disorder* of later childhood—phobic type, acute, severe, manifested by fear of school, separation anxiety and morning nausea.

5. *Personality disorder* of later childhood—compulsive type, chronic, moderate, manifested by ritualistic behavior, counting compulsions, and obsessive rumination.

6. *Psychotic disorder* of later childhood—schizophreniform type, chronic, severe, manifested by autistic behavior, associative (thought) disorder, resistance to change, whirling, echolalia, ritualistic behavior, and panic states.

7a. *Psychophysiologic skin disorder* of later childhood— chronic, moderate, manifested by neurodermatitis and excoriations.

  b. *Personality disorder*—overly inhibited type, chronic, severe, manifested by withdrawn behavior, learning inhibition, and hesitant speech.

8. *Brain syndrome* of early childhood—chronic, moderate, manifested by hyperkinesis, impulsive behavior, distractibility, and difficulties in coordinaton.

9a. *Mental retardation* of adolescence—chronic, mild.

  b. *Psychotic disorder*—schizophrenic type, chronic, moderate, manifested by autistic behavior, associative (thought) disorder, and continuing enuresis.

3

PROPOSED CLASSIFICATION

The following major categories are proposed:
1. Healthy Responses
2. Reactive Disorders
3. Developmental Deviations
4. Psychoneurotic Disorders
5. Personality Disorders
6. Psychotic Disorders
7. Psychophysiologic Disorders
8. Brain Syndromes
9. Mental Retardation
10. Other Disorders

These categories are arranged rather arbitrarily and roughly in a hierarchy ranging from healthy responses, through milder to more severe psychological disorders, to syndromes in which somatic factors predominate. The placing of the healthier or the less disturbed groups at the top of this hierarchical arrangement reflects in general the degree of optimism of the Committee regarding the prognostic outlook in childhood, with significant exceptions. The considerations mentioned earlier regarding total personality responses, contrasted with end-organ patterns or specific etiological influences, also apply. A list of the major categories and the proposed subcategories follows.

1. Healthy Responses
   a. Developmental crisis
   b. Situational crisis
   c. Other responses

217

2. Reactive Disorders
3. Developmental Deviations
    a. Deviations in maturational patterns
    b. Deviations in specific dimensions of development
        1) Motor
        2) Sensory
        3) Speech
        4) Cognitive functions
        5) Social development
        6) Psychosexual
        7) Affective
        8) Integrative
    c. Other developmental deviation
4. Psychoneurotic Disorders
    a. Anxiety type
    b. Phobic type
    c. Conversion type
    d. Dissociative type
    e. Obsessive-compulsive type
    f. Depressive type
    g. Other psychoneurotic disorder
5. Personality Disorders
    a. Compulsive personality
    b. Hysterical
    c. Anxious
    d. Overly dependent
    e. Oppositional
    f. Overly inhibited
    g. Overly independent
    h. Isolated
    i. Mistrustful
    j. Tension-discharge disorders
        1) Impulse-ridden personality
        2) Neurotic personality disorder
    k. Sociosyntonic personality disorder

l. Sexual deviation

m. Other personality disorder

6. Psychotic Disorders

  a. Psychoses of infancy and early childhood

    1) Early infantile autism

    2) Interactional psychotic disorder

    3) Other psychosis of infancy and early childhood

  b. Psychoses of later childhood

    1) Schizophreniform psychotic disorder

    2) Other psychosis of later childhood

  c. Psychoses of adolescence

    1) Acute confusional state

    2) Schizophrenic disorder, adult type

    3) Other psychosis of adolescence

7. Psychophysiologic Disorders

  a. Skin

  b. Musculoskeletal

  c. Respiratory

  d. Cardiovascular

  e. Hemic and lymphatic

  f. Gastrointestinal

  g. Genitourinary

  h. Endocrine

  i. Of nervous system

  j. Of organs of special sense

  k. Other psychophysiologic disorders

8. Brain Syndromes

  a. Acute

  b. Chronic

9. Mental Retardation

10. Other Disorders

1. Healthy Responses

This category is presented as the first on the list in order to emphasize the need for the assessment of positive strengths in the child wherever possible and to avoid so far as possible the diagnosis of healthy states by the exclusion of pathology. The relativity of states of health and disease and of the definition of normality was mentioned earlier in regard to the current state of adaptation and development in one individual compared to another and in relation to cross-cultural considerations. Although the criteria for the assessment of healthy responses are still somewhat subjective and impressionistic, a positive assessment can be made at least in terms of part functions and their relation to total functioning, allowing for developmental level.

These criteria cover *intellectual functioning,* involving adequate use of capacity, intact memory, reality-testing ability, age-appropriate thought processes, some degree of inquisitiveness, alertness, and imagination; *social functioning,* involving an adequate balance between dependent and independent strivings, reasonable comfort and appropriate love in relationships with other children and adults (including family "fit," role acceptance, tolerance, and cooperation with other members), and age-appropriate capacities to share and to empathize with peer-group representatives; *emotional functioning,* involving general mood quality, some degree of stability of emotional responses, some capacity for self-perspective, some degree of frustration tolerance, sublimation potential, and some capacity to master anxiety and to deal with conflicting emotions; *personal and adaptive functioning,* involving a degree of flexibility, drive toward mastery, coping capacities, and adaptive or integrative capacity, the latter making possible the balanced use of defenses, some degree of self-awareness, the existence of a self-concept, the capacity to use fantasy in play in constructive fashion, and other criteria.

The application of such positive personality criteria would appear in the present state of our knowledge to be more appropriate than reliance upon the presence of such mental states as contentment, happiness, and freedom from fear or inhibition or reliance upon the existence of certain personality patterns or traits. The age-appropriateness or, better, *stage-appropriateness* of functioning is a basic consideration, as are the balance of progressive versus regressive forces and the general "smoothness" of development. The latter includes an assessment by the clinician of the child in the present, his mastery of stresses in the past, and the feel of the future in a long-term assessment. The distinction between adjustment and adaptation from maturity or creativity, discussed in the introductory section, is pertinent here.

The child's or adolescent's *psychosocial functioning* (degree of trust, autonomy, initiative, industry, identity, intimacy, etc.) are included among these criteria. It is recognized that such criteria may be modified in accordance with the child's endowment, his current developmental level, the nature of the stresses to which he is subjected in his particular family and social setting, and other factors, among them the appropriateness of his behavior in a particular configurational setting.

Within this category can be grouped certain *developmental crises,* of brief and presumably transient nature, related to the child's attempt to complete successfully such psychosocial tasks as the establishment of trust, autonomy, initiative, industry, and identity. The so-called eighth-month anxiety, related to beginning individuation; the separation anxiety of the young preschool child; the normal phobias of the older preschool child struggling with the need to develop initiative and sexual identity; the so-called compulsive or ritualistic behavior of the school-age child working on a sense of industry, and the identity crisis of the adolescent—all could be included here among such considerations, together with varying degrees of mild regressive or other adaptive maneuvers employed. These latter should be specified from the Symptom List (anxiety, thumb-sucking, etc.).

Transient *situational crises* would also be noted in this category, for example, the "work of mourning" in the healthy grief reaction, and other responses which are considered to be normal adaptive responses and not disturbed behavior. Specific behaviors should be drawn from the Symptom List. The distinction between developmental and situational crises may be a fine one at times. The balance between internal and external forces is significant, however, with internal forces predominating in developmental crises. Healthy responses may, through parental unawareness or overconcern, evolve into significant developmental deviations, reactive disorders, or other conditions. Also parental overconcern or lack of knowledge of expected behavior at a particular level of development may lead parents to misperceive healthy behavior as pathological.

Under "Other responses" can be placed developmental variations within the healthy range relating to differing dimensions of development. If the clinician wishes to employ any available typology of healthy personality functioning, this could be included here, with appropriate subcategories.

2. Reactive Disorders

This category should be used for those disorders in which the behavior and/or symptoms shown by the child are judged to be primarily a reaction to an event, a set of events, or a situation. Such disturbances must be considered to be of pathological degree, thus distinguishing them from situational crises in the category of healthy responses. The disorder is a manifestation of a predominantly conscious conflict between the child's drives and feelings and his social environment and does not represent an unconscious internalized process. This category is to be distinguished from disorders secondary to congenital defect and from developmental deviations; it does not include those disorders which have developed into a structuralized psychoneurosis, a personality disorder with fixed patterns, or a psychosis. A reactive disorder may, however, be superimposed upon any of these disorders.

A careful evaluation of the child in his social environment is necessary to make the diagnosis of reactive disorder. It should be based on positive criteria and should not be made by exclusion. It must be demonstrated that a situation exists, that it is emotionally traumatic for the particular child, and that the reaction is causally related to the specific event or situation, not just coincident with it.

A great variety of events or situations (e.g., illness, accident or hospitalization; loss of a parent; the attitudes and/or behavior of others, particularly parents; school pressures; or premature, excessive or inadequate stimulation) may precipitate or perpetuate a reactive disorder. The effect of the situation is in part dependent upon the degree of its acuteness or chronicity: A situation arising suddenly may have a profound effect, while a more gradual evolution may allow the child sufficient time for mastery—it may be tolerated for a short period but not if it is prolonged.

In making the diagnosis of reactive disorder, the dynamic state and reaction of the child should be emphasized rather than the degree of stress. Some situations might be judged to be potentially traumatic for all or most children. Yet relatively mild stimuli may produce a reactive disorder in a particular child, depending upon its meaning to the child and to his parents, the nature of his past experiences, his original endowment, his level of development, and the adaptive resources he has available. Reactions to illness or hospitalization may depend more upon the young child's misinterpretation of the experience than upon actual events. A situation which will have a profound effect upon an infant may have little effect upon an older child. On the other hand, the impact may depend on the child's having reached a certain level of development.

The nature of the reaction is again dependent upon the child's endowment, the stage and extent of his development, his personality tendencies, his past experiences, and his resources. The reaction may take the form of arrest in development or of a variety of symptoms, psychological manifestations or behavioral aberrations. Part of the reaction may represent adaptive attempts, as in regression or withdrawal, while part may be a sign of adaptive failure, as in marked anorexia. Physiologic concomitants of emotions may be involved, or a psychophysiologic part disorder may be triggered during the reactive process.

The infant suddenly deprived of adequate mothering may react with apathy, eating and sleeping disturbances and failure to thrive. The older child may react with disturbances in conduct and may try to punish or coerce his environment by active aggressive behavior or by passive resistance. He may withdraw into himself for solace, developing habit patterns such as thumb-sucking or manipulating parts of his body. He may continue infantile patterns or regress to them, as with wetting or soiling. He may show overt panic or other psychological reactions, such as excessive daydreaming and preoccupation with fantasy. At times a child may identify with a seriously disturbed or psychotic parent or sibling and show similar symptoms or behavior without psychosis. Such a *folie a deux* may represent a reactive disorder on the part of the child if it has not progressed to the point where such characteristics have become fixed traits in a chronic personality disorder or other disturbance.

Reactive disorders can occur at any age but are more likely to be seen in infants and preschool children because they are less likely to have the capacity to repress affect, internalize conflict, and develop a structured psychopathology. The developmental capacities of the child will operate as a major determinant of the reactive picture; additional determinants will be the way in which the family and others handle the reaction, the nature of the precipitating stresses, and other forces. The behavior and/or symptoms should be specified with the use of the Symptom List, and the reactive disorder should be indicated as occurring in infancy, early childhood, later childhood, or adolescence. If the reactive disorder is superimposed upon one of the other clinical disorders such as a personality disorder, this should be indicated, with an additional diagnosis.

The outcome of the reactive disorders, with or without treatment, can, like that of other disorders, only be ascertained by follow-up. Although the majority of these disorders may be transient or temporary, a variety of forces can lead to more chronically incapacitating pictures—for example, structuralized traumatic neuroses.

Under reactive disorders would be classified a number of diagnostic entities referred to in the literature. These would include behavior disorders, conduct disturbances, neurotic traits, habit disturbances, and anaclitic depression, among others.

3. Developmental Deviations

This category is intended to delineate those deviations in personality development which may be considered beyond the range of normal variation in that they occur at a time, in a sequence, or in a degree not expected for a given age level or stage of development. A developmental crisis appearing very early or very late may represent such a deviation. Developmental deviations are not necessarily of fixed nature: The passage of time, the process of working through, or minimal help from parents or other external figures may lead to their correction. In certain instances, depending upon the way the child is handled later or upon other extraneous or intrinsic influences, the deviation may represent the premonitory stages of a more structured disorder and can be differentiated only by follow-up or continued evaluation.

Biological (hereditary, constitutional, or maturational) factors are conceived of as contributing prominently to developmental deviations. Some modification or intensification may result from experience, however, as the result of family interactions, emotional deprivation and other factors, while an earlier, unresolved reactive disorder may represent a predisposing influence. Deviations of predominantly physical nature, such as delayed growth, precocious puberty, or delayed menstruation, should be given a primary diagnosis drawn from the Standard Nomenclature. A secondary diagnosis should be given in such instances, indicating the child's reaction to the physiologic deviation—whether a healthy response, reactive disorder, or psychoneurotic disorder. In those instances where psychological factors may play an important role in disturbances of physical parameters of development (as in delayed growth or delay in onset of menstruation) these would probably best be classified under the heading of psychophysiologic disorders, with an accompanying personality diagnosis.

In classifying developmental deviations, certain considerations mentioned earlier regarding total and part functions apply. Many deviations appear to involve almost the total maturational timetable or a number of part functions, while others apply only to individual aspects of development. To deal with such variations, the broader category of deviations in maturational patterns has been employed. Certain major parameters or part functions of personality development have been listed separately to cover those children whose deviations lie predominantly within these dimensions. Where more than one major parameter is involved, as may often be the case, these can be specified, or the broader category may be employed. In children with deviations in a single dimension such as motor or sensory, an associated personality disorder or other total personality disturbance may later develop; where this is the case, the personality disturbance should be specified as the primary diagnosis, with the developmental deviation listed secondarily.

In those instances where other features may be present which are not listed in the classification, the category of *other developmental deviation* can be utilized, with any subheadings the clinician wishes to employ. In all instances the diagnosis should be qualified by the specific behavioral manifestation(s) drawn from the Symptom List. Where appropriate, the accelerated, delayed, or uneven nature of the disorder should be noted. The use of this category demands detailed knowledge of the expected behavior for different levels of development; it should not be used as a wastebasket.

a. Deviations in Maturational Patterns

These include the broader, almost total lags, sweeping unevennesses, or precocities in maturational steps mentioned. They would also apply to children with deviations in their capacities for attainment of control or rhythmic integration in such bodily functions as sleeping, eating, speech, bowel or bladder functions.

b. Deviations in Specific Dimensions of Development

1) *Deviations in motor development* include long-continued deviations in psychomotor functions and activity levels (hyperactivity, hypoactivity), and deviations in coordination, handed-

ness, and other predominantly motoric capacities in which brain damage or other factors do not appear to be involved. Some hyperkinetic children without brain damage would be considered in this category; other deviations, where anxiety produces the hyperactivity, would be classified under reactive disorders or under appropriate total personality categories, with the hyperactivity listed as a symptom.

2) *Deviations in sensory development* include difficulties in monitoring stimuli, from tactile to social in nature. Children with such difficulties may respond overreactively to ordinary sensory input by becoming easily overstimulated, or may show underreactive or uneven responses. Manifest behavior in response to stimuli may range from difficulties in falling asleep to exhibitionistic, regressive, or apathetic behavior and should be specified from the Symptom List.

3) *Deviations in speech development* would include significant delays in speech development other than those based on deafness, oppositional behavior, elective mutism, brain damage, or early childhood psychosis. Certain children with disorders of articulation, rhythm, phonation, or comprehension of speech of a persistently infantile type, without somatic abnormality, could also be placed in this category, as well as those with marked precocity in speech development. The normal repetition of words by a healthy child in the early preschool phase and stuttering as a conversion symptom should be distinguished from some deviations in this group.

4) *Deviations in cognitive functions* include developmental lags or other deviations in the capacity for symbolic or abstract thinking, among these the functions of reading, writing, and working arithmetic problems. Some children may exhibit the persistence of prelogical thought processes or a delay in repression of primitive fantasies, as well as other deviations in cerebral integration unrelated to brain damage. In this category would be certain children referred to as pseudoretarded and possibly, as well, some children who may be mildly retarded in mental development at the lower end of the normal distribution curve

of intellectual potential rather than retarded because of inborn, inherent, or extrinsic defects in intellectual functioning. Children who are significantly precocious or accelerated in their intellectual development can also be considered in this category.

5) *Deviations in social development* include precocious, delayed or uneven patterns of social capacities or relationships which have not crystallized into true personality disorders. Delayed achievement of autonomy in the capacity for separation from the parent, marked shyness, dependence, inhibitions, and immaturely aggressive behavior are examples.

6) *Deviations in psychosexual development* include significant deviations in the timing of appearance of sexual curiosity, the persistence of infantile autoerotic patterns or markedly precocious or delayed heterosexual interests. Also included would be deviations in heterosexual identifications, as with more passive-feminine boys or somewhat masculine girls who do not show actual sexual inversion or perversion. They may exhibit some internalized conflict without the presence of a psychoneurosis or personality disorder. Passive-feminine boys in particular may develop learning inhibitions; this can be listed as one of the manifestations, using the Symptom List.

7) *Deviations in affective development* include such patterns as moderately anxious tendencies, emotional lability of a type less mature than the child's level of development would ordinarily involve, marked overcontrol of affect inappropriate to the stage, mildly depressed or apathetic tendencies, or other affective trends of continued nature which do not involve structured psychoneurotic reactions or personality disorders. Children with cyclic patterns of behavior resembling euphoria and hypomanic activity, alternating with some depressed moods and diminished activity, should also be considered in this category.

8) *Deviations in integrative development* include moderate deviations in the development of impulse controls or frustration tolerance and the uneven or overactive use of certain defense mechanisms, such as projection or denial, without the presence of personality disorder or psychosis.

c. *Other Developmental Deviations*

These would include any specific deviations in development considered of significance by the reporting clinician but not specified within the two preceding developmental subcategories.

4. Psychoneurotic Disorders

This category is reserved for those disorders based on unconscious conflicts over the handling of sexual and aggressive impulses which, though removed from awareness by the mechanism of repression, remain active and unresolved. Such neurotic conflicts are ordinarily derived from earlier conscious conflicts between the child and significant persons in his environment such as parents and siblings. Thus they have their genesis in the preschool years, during the time of the child's involvement in the issues of personality individuation, early sex identification, and social integration. During this earlier period, various symptomatic reactions may be observed, that may fluctuate and change. In older children, the neurotic conflicts are internalized; since the organism is still in process of development, however, modification may still occur, leading to the prevalence of symptomatology at certain stages and to shifts in the symptomatic picture.

Marked personality disorganization or decompensation is not seen in these disorders, although some regression is common; they are relatively encapsulated and the child's reality testing is not grossly disturbed. Because of their internalized character, they tend toward chronicity, with a self-perpetuating or repetitive nature. However, the prognosis for response to treatment is generally good. Some mild psychoneurotic disorders may resolve spontaneously as the child later reworks the conflicts at a higher level of maturation, permitting him to resolve developmental tasks which he was previously unable to master.

Conflicts which the individual is unable to resolve but attempts to handle neurotically through overstrenuous repression characteristically arouse anxiety; this is perceived by the conscious portion of the personality and may produce an unconscious pathological association of ideas, affects, and events. The anxiety, acting as a danger signal to the ego, ordinarily sets into operation certain defense mechanisms, in addition to repression, and leads to the formation of psychological symptoms which symbolically deal with the conflict, thus achieving a partial though unhealthy solution. The symptom is at times recognized by the child as something foreign and painful (ego-alien) over which he has no control; this awareness is less consistent in children, particularly in the early stages, than in adults.

Fully structured psychoneurotic disorders do not ordinarily occur until the early school-age period, by which time the child's personality structure is sufficiently crystallized developmentally to permit operation of the conscience or superego, the internalization of conflict, the removal or repression of affects from awareness, the appearance of various defense mechanisms, and the process of symptom formation with its symbolic significance. Repression may occur earlier, however, and some symptoms arising in reactive disorders in the preschool child may have unconscious symbolic significance. Individual psychoneurotic symptoms of symbolic nature may thus occasionally be seen as early as the third or fourth year. Often the diagnosis will be difficult to make and may have to be altered *a posteriori*, depending upon the trends in meaning and evolution of the symbolic process with relation to the child's further development. The differential diagnosis must cover reactive disorders, developmental deviations, crises within healthy development, and some predominantly physical disorders as, for example, thyrotoxicosis and certain paralyses, which psychoneurotic disorders, of the anxiety and conversion types particularly, may resemble to some extent symptomatically.

Precursors of the neurotic picture may be unresolved developmental or situational crises in healthy children which may become intensified in the face of unhealthy reactions or conflicts on the part of the parents, with the later appearance of psychoneurotic disorders. Reactive disorders may also be followed by internalization of conflict and the development of a structuralized psychoneurosis in the light of later precipitating external events intensifying the neurotic conflict and producing a shift in the adaptive equilibrium, calling out the clinical picture.

In certain instances, the precipitating situational stress, with all its relativity and individualized meaning, may be so overwhelming and unexpected to the child as to produce a traumatic neurosis. If, as often occurs, this picture is due to the sudden crystallization of a latent or subclinical psychoneurotic disorder, it should be classified under the heading of the appropriate psychoneurotic subtype. If such is not the case, it may be classified as a severe reactive disorder.

In some cases, for reasons which are not completely clear, symptom formation may not occur. The personality structure of the child may be affected by neurotic conflicts, altering the patterns of reaction to internal demands and adaptation to the environment. These may assume the character of personality traits, which ordinarily cause little or no conscious anxiety (egosyntonic), as with some types of aggressive or acting-out behavior that have symbolic significance. When these become fully established as personality disorders, they should be classified under the latter heading.

Children with true psychoneurotic disorders may show disturbances in behavior, in addition to symbolic symptoms. Although they are not ordinarily openly aggressive, often fearing loss of control of their own aggressive impulses, aggressive behavior related to fears of harm or attack may occur. Hyperactivity, usually of intermittent nature, may also be seen in such children, particularly those with psychoneurotic pictures of the anxiety type. When such associated manifestations of behavioral disturbance occur, they can be specified with the use of the Symptom List.

Mixed psychoneurotic disorders, which are common in children, should be classified according to the predominant feature, with a qualifying statement as to the existence of trends of another subtype. Individual symptoms may be further specified with entries drawn from the Symptom List.

a. Psychoneurotic Disorder, Anxiety Type

In these pictures, the anxiety arising from the unconscious internalized conflict appears to break through into awareness as an intense and diffuse feeling of apprehension or impending disaster, in contrast to normal apprehensions, conscious fears or content-specific phobias. The anxiety is ordinarily free-floating in nature, without the appearance of stable defense mechanisms or symbolic symptom formation, and it may arise in a variety of situations. Physiologic concomitants of anxiety are commonly present in varying degree. These do not lead to structural change in the organ systems involved, by contrast with psychophysiologic disorders.

In children, anxiety neuroses are not apt to remain in a diffuse state but will often develop into one of the more crystallized "symptom" neuroses. Anxiety neuroses are to be distinguished from acute panic states, which should ordinarily be classified as reactive disorders.

b. Psychoneurotic Disorder, Phobic Type

Into this category fall psychoneurotic disorders in which the child has unconsciously displaced the content of his original conflict onto an object or a situation in the external environment that has symbolic significance for him. The fears generated by the unconscious internal conflict break through into consciousness but are distorted and irrational. Thus the child avoids those objects and situations that revive or intensify his displaced conflict, and he frequently projects his unacceptable feelings onto the external feared object or situation. He may show a conscious fear of animals, school, dirt, disease, high places, elevators, and the like.

Developmental crises involving separation anxiety, with concern for the whereabouts of the mother, should be distinguished from phobic disorders such as school phobias, with their internalized and structured character. The mild fears and transient phobias of the healthy preschool child and the fears of specifically stressful experiences in reactive disorders, as in the young child who fears persons in white coats following hospitalization, should also be recognized as distinct from neurotic phobic disorders. The specific content of the phobic disorder should be specified, with the use of the Symptom List, as "manifested by fear of school," ". . . animals," and so on.

c. Psychoneurotic Disorder, Conversion Type

In these disorders, the original conflict appears to be dealt with unconsciously, after repression, through a conversion centrally into a somatic dysfunction, involving a disturbance in function of bodily structures or organs supplied by the voluntary portion of the central nervous system. Such dysfunctions thus ordinarily involve the striated musculature and the somatosensory apparatus. Conversion disorders may produce disturbances in motor function, as in paralysis or motor tics; alterations in sensory perception, as in cases of blindness or deafness; disturbances in awareness, as in conversion syncope or convulsive-like phenomena; and disturbances in the total body image, as in psychological invalidism associated with intense weakness, bizarre paralyses, or other symptoms. They may also produce disturbances in function of the upper and lower ends of the gastrointestinal tract, as in certain types of vomiting or encopresis; the voluntary components of respiration, as in hyperventilation, respiratory or barking tics; and the genitourinary organs, as in certain types of enuresis or bladder atony, in all of which structures voluntary innervation is at least partially involved. Unusual combinations of conversion symptoms may occur, as in the *maladie des tics*. Children with such disorders often show marked degrees of personality malfunctioning bordering on psychosis and, when they do, should be given a personality diagnosis of severe personality disorder or psychosis, with the conversion disorder listed as a secondary diagnosis.

In conversion disorders, the symptom appears symbolically to express the conflict, and a partial solution results, at the cost of illness and suffering but with unconscious secondary gain accruing from enhanced dependence or other sources. The anxiety aroused by the conflict appears to be bound to the bodily symptom, and little conscious concern is present. The psychological determinants of the symptom may vary, from a type of "organ language" to identification with the symptom of a parent, the memory of a traumatic experience, or the unconscious need for punishment. The disturbance in function does not follow anatomical lines of distribution but conforms to the child's unconscious need and his naive concepts of bodily function. Transient conversion symptomatology may occur in reaction to specific situational stresses in children, including convalescence from physical illness, without the character of fixed conversion disorders. In adolescents and adults, conversion disorders frequently occur in hysterical personalities, most common in women but appearing also in men. They may appear in other personality pictures, however, and this is particularly so in childhood.

In classifying a disorder in this category, the individual symptoms should be specified, as drawn from the Symptom List. Certain symptoms, although involving voluntarily innervated structures, may not partake of the symbolic significance of true conversion disorders. This is the case with rumination, aerophagia, and eructatio nervosa in infants and with certain regressive manifestations such as the temporary giving up of walking or talking in older infants and very young children. These symptoms ordinarily occur in the context of a reactive disorder of infancy or early childhood and are best classified under such a heading. Similar symptoms in older children may represent conversion phenomena and can be dealt with as such.

When conversion disorders occur in an individual with other than a hysterical personality, the appropriate personality diagnosis should also be specified. Conversion disorders must be distinguished principally from symptoms of predominantly physical illness and psychophysiologic disorders; these may at times be admixed, in varying combinations, and multiple diagnoses should be employed where necessary.

d. Psychoneurotic Disorder, Dissociative Type

In this category should be classified disorders based on neurotic conflicts that lead to some temporary general personality disorganization, with repressed impulses or affects giving rise to anxiety which results in aimless motor discharge or "freezing," fugue states, catalepsy, cataplexy, transient catatonic states without underlying psychosis, and other pictures. The self-representation of the personality may be disturbed; depersonalization, dissociated personality, amnesia, and, in adolescents, the Ganser syndrome and pseudopsychotic states or "hysterical psychoses" may be present episodically. Disturbances in consciousness may occur, with hypnogogic and hypnopompic or so-called twilight states, marked somnambulism, pseudodelirious and stuporous states, and certain types of narcolepsy resulting.

These disorders, like conversion disorders, often occur in hysterical personalities; they may appear in other psychopathologic disorders as well, and, rarely, isolated symptoms of some of these types may occur transiently in healthy children as the result of overwhelmingly stressful situations. Other total personality diagnoses should thus be specified when appropriate. Diagnosis should indicate the symptomatic manifestations and should be differentiated from psychotic disorders and epileptic equivalents, among other entities.

e. Psychoneurotic Disorder, Obsessive-Compulsive Type

In these disorders, the anxiety aroused by the unconscious conflict is counteracted by the occurrence of thoughts (obsessions) or acts or impulses to act (compulsions), or mixtures of both, that are isolated from the original unacceptable impulse. The child frequently recognizes his ideas or behavior as being unreasonable but is nevertheless compelled to repeat his rituals. Often the external behavior represents the opposite of the unconscious wish, as with excessive orderliness and washing compulsions overlying impulses to soil or to mess. Counting and touching ceremonials frequently appear, with marked anxiety resulting if they are interfered with by the parents or other persons.

These disorders must be distinguished from normal compulsive-like or ritualistic behavior such as the ritual formations in early childhood around sleeping or training habits or the repetition compulsions and rituals in the early school-age child seen in games or other activities and carried on in the service of attaining mastery over impulses of an aggressive nature. The specific symptom patterns should be indicated from the Symptom List.

f. Psychoneurotic Disorder, Depressive Type
Depression in children and even in adolescents may be manifested in ways somewhat different from those manifested by adults. These include eating and sleeping disturbances, hyperactivity, and other patterns. The picture of depression may be much more clear and marked, particularly when precipitated by an actual, threatened, or symbolic loss of a parent or parent substitute. Loss of self-esteem, feelings of self-depreciation, guilt, and ambivalence toward the loved person may be present in older children, as in adults. However, psychomotor retardation is ordinarily less marked than in adults, and, except in young infants, the same is true of some of the other biologic signs of depression.

Psychoneurotic depressive disorders of a more chronic nature, involving internalized conflicts in relation to deeply ambivalent feelings, are only rarely seen in children at peak intensity, as they and their equivalents are characteristically modified by the child's stage of development. When they occur, they are to be distinguished from more acute reactive disorders in which depression may be involved, as in the anaclitic type. Such disorders should also be separated from fleeting feelings of depression in healthy children undergoing developmental or situational crises; from cyclical behavioral and mood swings as occasionally seen in developmental deviations; and from psychotic depressive pictures, which are seen at times in adolescents with schizoaffective disorders more similar to adult pictures.

Suicidal threats may be made by depressed children, as well

as by children with other types of disorders, particularly reactive disorders. They may be seen in normal children under particularly stressful circumstances. Serious suicidal attempts do not ordinarily occur until adolescence, however; and even then they may have a different, more temporary character than adult suicidal pictures, with more of the element of a cry for help. If suicidal threats or attempts occur, these should be classified under the appropriate personality heading, with the specified behavior drawn from the Symptom List.

g. Other Psychoneurotic Disorder

Under this category can be placed any disorders considered to be of psychoneurotic nature that do not fit into the specific group categories—for example, certain cases of traumatic neurosis. Mixed neurotic disorders, as mentioned earlier, should be classified under the predominant heading, as in the Standard Nomenclature, with a statement regarding manifestations of other types. Manifestations of identification of a child with a neurotic parent would be classified usually under the heading of reactive disorder or of developmental deviation. Hypochondriacal behavior in children is ordinarily seen as a reactive disorder or as part of a psychotic picture. So-called kleptomaniac behavior usually would be classified, under the heading of personality disorder, as a personality trait influenced by prior neurotic conflicts.

5. Personality Disorders

These disorders are characterized by chronic or fixed pathological trends, representing traits which have become ingrained in the personality structure. Symptom formation of a psychoneurotic nature is rarely seen, although earlier neurotically repressed conflicts may have led to the patterns of response which have crystallized into the specific personality or behavioral traits manifested. In most but not all such disorders, these trends or traits are not perceived by the child as a source of intrapsychic distress or anxiety and can be said to be ego-syntonic. For developmental reasons, as discussed earlier, these disorders are not seen commonly in structured form until the later school-age period. Nevertheless, the developmental experiences which contribute to their genesis, together with constitutional and other factors, are often found to occur during infancy and early childhood, and premonitory patterns are often seen.

In discussing these disorders, the concept of a continuum is useful. At one end are relatively well-organized personalities with, for example, constructively compulsive traits or somewhat overdependent characteristics, representing mild to moderate exaggeration of healthy personality trends. These may blend into their environment and may almost pass unnoticed unless the interpersonal network of relationships suddenly or radically changes. At the other end are markedly impulsive, sometimes poorly organized personalities that dramatically come into conflict with society over their sexual or social patterns of behavior. Marked regression may arise in some of these disorders without evidence of true psychosis. In some severe forms, however, signs of an associated thought disorder may be present and a psychotic disorder may occasionally supervene. In milder forms, decompensation in the face of external stress may occasionally ensue, with the appearance of neurotic symptom formation superimposed upon the basic personality picture. A reactive disorder may also occur in a child with a chronic personality disorder. Most personality disorders appear to involve strong fixations in psychosexual and psychosocial development at infancy and early childhood levels, related to original conflicts over the handling of dependent wishes, strivings for autonomy, the handling of aggressive impulses, and sexual differentiation.

In classifying disorders under this heading, the total personality picture should be considered and not the presence of a single symptom or behavioral characteristic such as hyperactivity, enuresis, or shyness. These latter should be included as individual symptoms or traits from the Symptom List, placed under the appropriate personality heading, whether developmental deviation, reactive disorder, or other. Mixed personality disorders do not occur uncommonly; these should be classified according to the predominant set of personality patterns, with a statement regarding the existence of trends or features of another type.

The subcategories proposed herein are somewhat different from those now employed in the Standard Nomenclature. These differences arise in part from the more shifting nature of childhood disturbances, with the possibility of significant change during adolescence, and in part from certain conceptual considerations. "Special symptom disturbances," for example, are common in children but are viewed as part disturbances; they should be drawn from the Symptom List, with appropriate classification under the total personality heading of reactive disorder, developmental deviation, or other deviation. They should be classified with personality disorders only when they occur as part of a total personality picture. Emotionally unstable, inadequate, immature behavior, as well as demanding, controlling, or narcissistic trends, among others, are of course common features in childhood disorders and indeed may occur in healthy responses of young children. Where these are considered pathological, they are ordinarily not the dominant structural characteristics and thus should be classified as symptoms under the heading of developmental deviations or reactive disorders.

Addiction to drugs, alcohol, or other substances, as in glue-sniffing, although seen in older children and adolescents, is also conceived ordinarily as an individual symptomatic manifestation or trait, to be specified from the Symptom List in relation to the basic personality disorder of overdependent, impulse-ridden, or other nature. Disorders such as the cyclothymic personality, where they occur in childhood, are probably best listed under developmental deviations in affective development, rather than as a separate personality disorder; if they appear to be entities, they can be placed in the category of *Other personality disorder*. Sexual deviations or so-called perversions can be listed in this category when they appear to have become the dominant trend in the total personality. In childhood, however, sexually deviant behavior is common, and ordinarily it would seem more appropriate to specify the sexual behavior as a part of the basic personality picture, whatever that may be. For example, some sexual deviations which appear to be related to delay, acceleration, or unevenness in psychosexual aspects of development should be classified under the heading of developmental deviations. Others may be normal for the stage of development, or they may be part of reactive, psychoneurotic, psychotic disorders, or various personality disorders.

As indicated earlier, stress reactions, in the conceptual framework employed, are viewed generally as reactive disorders. Emphasis is laid upon the child's reaction, in the face of the relativity of stressful stimuli and the ready confusion between the stimulus and the response which is implicit in the word *stress*. Adjustment reactions, also for reasons of conceptual clarity, are subsumed herein under healthy responses, in relation to developmental or situational crises; or under reactive disorders. The following subcategories of personality disorders are proposed for the childhood age range.

a. Compulsive Personality

These children show chronic and excessive concern with orderliness, cleanliness, and conformity. Their personalities are ordinarily relatively rigid and inflexible, with difficulties in achieving relaxation. When their patterns are disrupted, they may be aware of some tension or anxiety but they usually perceive their environment or other persons as being responsible for their distress. They may have some obsessive thoughts and compulsive rituals but only rarely decompensate, in the face of increased conflict and anxiety, to the point where these become crippling neurotic symptoms. Ordinarily they perform well and frequently show a kind of pseudomaturity, with the sort of lively affectivity ordinarily associated by many adults with what they presume to be healthy childhood behavior.

b. Hysterical Personality

This group of children, mostly girls but including some boys, shows tendencies toward overdramatic, flamboyant, overlabile, overaffective, oversuggestible, coy, or seductive behavior. They often appear to be overly dependent upon their environment for the establishment of their own independent identities and may exhibit a pseudosocial poise or veneer. Despite their often misleading overt heterosexual behavior, they give evidence of unusual repression of sexual impulses and of difficulties in the establishment of their sexual identities and relationships. Masochistic needs for the experiencing of suffering or pain may be present unconsciously. Symptom formation of conversion or dissociative nature may occur at times of increased conflict, though rarely in individuals with milder hysterical personality disorders. In more severe instances, a variety of shifting symptoms may occur, with psychological invalidism reflecting deep disturbance in body-image formation.

Individuals in this category may be strongly manipulative or demanding in a passive-aggressive fashion, indicating that fixations of conflict at very early levels of personality development underlie the hysterical trends, which derive from a higher level of pseudosexual nature.

c. Anxious Personality

These children are chronically tense and apprehensive over new situations, often related to their extraordinarily vivid fantasies. They usually perceive the environment as threatening, however, and are not aware of and do not exhibit crippling anxiety, as do those with anxiety neurosis. Marked inhibitions or serious constriction of the total personality are not present, and they are often able to deal adequately with new situations after initial anxiety, in contrast to children with developmental deviations, who do not have stage-appropriate social capacities available.

d. Overly Dependent Personality

Such children are chronically helpless, clinging, and overdependent, with difficulties in achieving full autonomy and initiative. They may show markedly controlling or demanding behavior with passive-aggressive implications resembling an infantilized state. In this category would be included some children who formerly had to be classified as passive-aggressive personalities, as passive-dependent types, or as immature or unstable personalities.

e. Oppositional Personality

These children express their aggressiveness by oppositional patterns of generally passive character, although these patterns may have some actively aggressive implications. They may appear to be conforming, but they continually provoke adults or other children. By the use of negativism, stubbornness, dawdling, procrastination, and other measures, they covertly show their underlying aggressivity. Some passive-dependent or demanding trends may be present. If these oppositional tendencies invade the learning process, difficulties may arise from their patterns of blocking out, "failing to hear," or resisting passively external authority, which may lead to one form of learning difficulty. If present, the learning difficulty should be specified, as drawn from the Symptom List. At one level, these children may insist on their autonomy by negative adaptive maneuvers.

Children with these disorders previously had to classified as passive-aggressive personalities. They should be differentiated from children with developmental deviations and from children who act out their feelings aggressively in tension-discharge disorders. Individual characteristics of behavior should be specified from the Symptom List.

f. Overly Inhibited Personality

These children show superficial passivity, with extreme or "pathological" shyness, inhibition of motor action or initiative, and marked constriction of personality functions, including at times diminished speech or even elective mutism, among other features. They are distinguished from children with so-called schizoid (isolated) personalities by the fact that they seem to wish for warm and meaningful relationships but are inhibited from achieving them. They may be less inhibited in the home than at school or in other social settings. Some conscious anxiety may be evident, but the frozen, inhibited quality is ordinarily paramount. Some negativism and other oppositional features are frequently a part of the picture, although these do not seem to predominate, and such children exhibit considerable self-doubt and lack of achievement of autonomy.

Although their inhibitions, related primarily to unconscious fears of losing control of aggressive or sexual impulses, render these children somewhat dependent upon others for initial action, they are not ordinarily overdependent in many respects and may be able to function quite independently under special circumstances in which they have come to feel comfortable. Their inhibitions frequently spread over into areas of academic learning. There they may show difficulties in assimilating knowledge as well as in reproducing it, because of their fears of aggressive or competitive action and their constricted, unspontaneous personality trends.

Particular behavior, such as learning inhibition, elective mutism, etc., should be specified from the Symptom List.

g. Overly Independent Personality

Children in this category exhibit chronically ebullient, active, though not ordinarily hyperactive, behavior, with a need to rush toward independence and with difficulties in accepting teaching or the setting of limits by adult figures. Their behavior may have a pseudoprecocious or pseudoadult character, and they are ordinarily not aggressive in a destructive or antisocial sense.

Although such children may show some negativism, they are characterized by generally positive attitudes, with much impatience over growing up and, in some cases, a tendency toward overly responsible behavior of a pseudomature type. Many of them show a tendency to deny strongly feelings of helplessness or dependent needs. Some of them may be overcompensating for some fantasied defect or covering up fears of harm, injury, or anxiety arising from sexual conflicts. When physically ill, these children drive themselves too soon into full or overambitious activity or may otherwise experience difficulties in convalescence, with its enhancement of dependent needs and consequent conflicts over such gratifications. For some of them chronic illness or handicap may play a role in the genesis of their disorder.

h. Isolated Personality

Children in this category tend to exhibit distant, detached, cold, or withdrawn attitudes toward family and friends. Frequently they are isolated and seclusive or "isolating" persons; they experience difficulties in competition and in expression of even healthy aggressive impulses, although they may show occasional unpredictable outbursts of bizarrely aggressive or sadistic behavior.

Such children appear to differ quantitatively and qualitatively from overly inhibited personalities, having a restricted capacity for affective experience, in contrast to the inhibited children, who have the capacity for affective experience but encounter difficulties in expression. Shyness, oversensibility, inhibition, as well as passivity and some oppositional behavior, may be present, but the isolated child's inability to form warm and emotionally meaningful attachments is predominant. They appear to be introverted and withdrawn, uncommitted to warm relationships, overly satisfied with their isolation, with a rich fantasy life, and preoccupied with their own daydreams and autistic reveries, in contrast to the inhibited personality, which maintains relationships despite the difficulty in expressing affect.

Such isolated children are often quite capable of achieving successfully in certain areas of functioning, particularly intellectual areas, although many show mild deviations in thinking or concept formation without true thought disorder. They are generally pliant and unobtrusive in social situations; however, they may have occasional outbursts of aggressive, homicidal, or other negative behavior, unrelated to apparent stimuli from the external environment. There is a tendency for such children to show increased withdrawal and detachment in adolescence, as compared with others. Nevertheless only a small proportion appear to be definitely preschizophrenic, at least on the basis of clinical impression, and the picture does not seem to represent latent schizophrenia. For this reason the term *schizoid personality*, formerly often associated with latent or preschizophrenic tendencies, seems inappropriate, and the term *isolated personality* is employed. A constitutional tendency would seem likely in this picture, although this is not yet clear and early experience may play a significant role.

i. Mistrustful Personality

This disorder is seen rarely in childhood, appearing occasionally during late preadolescent or early adolescent phases. Such children may show some isolated features but are characterized by a pattern of suspiciousness (beyond the adolescent norm), with intense mistrust of others and marked rigidity of thinking. This latter involves heavy usage of projection but does not ordinarily progress to an actual paranoid state, as seen in adults. For this reason, the term *mistrustful personality* seems to the Committee to be preferable to *paranoid personality*. If the adult type is seen in late adolescence, that category can be utilized.

j. Tension-Discharge Disorders

Children in this category exhibit chronic behavioral patterns of emotional expression of aggressive and sexual impulses which conflict with society's norms. They act out directly their feelings or impulses toward persons or society in antisocial or destructive fashion, rather than inhibiting or repressing them and developing other modes of psychological defense or symptomatology. The terms, *antisocial personality, psychopathic personality, impulsive character,* and *sociopathic personality,* as well as *dyssocial personality, affectionless character, acting-out personality, neurotic character disorder, primary behavior disorder, neurotic behavior disorder,* and *conduct disorder,* have been used by different workers to designate differing individuals in this category, suggesting several subcategories.

In considering carefully this broad category, the Committee drew upon the basic conceptual framework set forth earlier. The terms, *psychopathic*, *sociopathic*, and *antisocial*, were felt to imply too fixed a pattern to apply to many children, even though such personality disorders may become chronic and difficult to treat by the late school age or early adolescent period. *Acting-out* seemed too broad a term; this pattern may occur in a variety of personality pictures or in different developmental phases, and the term is used differently by professional persons from differing conceptual backgrounds. To some, the term *character disorder* is inextricably entwined with moral judgments, which may not be appropriate clinically. *Conduct disorder* and *behavior disorder* seemed such broad terms as to have little meaning. *Primary behavior disorder* implies a type of distinction between primary and secondary etiologic factors that may be difficult to support in individual clinical situations.

Aggressive, destructive, or antisocial behavior may of course be seen in many children exhibiting reactive disorders, developmental deviations, or developmental crises in adolescence. Such behavior may occur as part of a picture involving brain damage, mental retardation, or a psychosis. Furthermore, some children in economically deprived urban areas may show behavior which is in conformity with the group code or mores of the neighborhood or gang but which is regarded as antisocial by society at large. Such children may function adequately in certain ways, however, and may show evidence of some conscience formation in their loyalty and codes of honor within their own groups. Many of them in later life can adjust their moral code, within limits, to that of society, although the possibility of continuing antisocial behavior is of course greater than in other categories.

Despite its dissatisfaction with many of the terms discussed in the foregoing, as they apply to children, the Committee felt that certain concepts were valuable and pertinent. The term *impulsive character* touches upon the central problem of difficulty in establishing impulse controls characteristic of certain of these children. The concept of *neurotic personality*, implying the existence of neurotic conflict underlying the behavior of other children, also seems clinically relevant, despite some terminological limitations. *Dyssocial* or *asocial*, while constructively implying the discrepancy between the child's local environment, where his behavior is appropriate, and that of society at large, seems to imply also some lack of capacity for socialization which may not at all be the case in terms of the child's relationships within his own subcultural group. Furthermore, the term *dyssocial* leaves little room for the child whose personality functioning is different from the majority because of his particular ethnic, racial, or other subcultural background—as in the child of a family from a society which utilizes magical concepts in its everyday thinking.

For these and other reasons, the Committee determined to employ the term *tension-discharge disorder* for the major category, with two subcategories subsuming the impulsive or impulse-ridden group and the group of children in whom neurotic conflicts seem to play so large a role. Tension-discharge disorder, while having limitations (as with any term), seemed to the Committee to convey best its conceptual recognition of the central tendency of these two groups, albeit from different sources, to discharge, rather than to delay or to inhibit, impulses unacceptable to the larger society. The group exhibiting deviant behavior on a subcultural basis was put into a separate major category of personality disorder (sociosyntonic); this was done to permit classification of children with various kinds of deviant personality patterns, over and beyond aggressive ones, and to emphasize the "fit" between the individual personality and the subcultural group, rather than the lack of capacity for socialization.

1) Impulse-ridden personality: These children show shallow relationships with adults or other children, having very low frustration tolerance. They exhibit great difficulty in control of their impulses, both aggressive and sexual, which are discharged immediately and impulsively, without delay or inhibition and often without any regard for the consequences. Little anxiety, internalized conflict, or guilt is experienced by most of these children, as the conflict remains largely external, between society and their impulses. (Some internalized conflict may be present, and some overlap exists among children with neurotic personality disorders.) The basic defect in impulse controls appears to be reinforced by a deficit in conscience or superego formation, with failure to develop the capacity for tension storage and for the postponement of gratifications. Such children ordinarily exhibit primitive defense mechanisms, with strong denial of dependent or other needs, projection of their hostile feelings onto adults or society, and rationalization of their own behavior.

Children in this category often have a history of extreme emotional deprivation during infancy and early childhood marked by frequent and prolonged separations from mothering figures. A large number of them come from lower socioeconomic or social class groups, although they may be found at any level of society. Some constitutional tendencies toward motoric discharge of tension rather than other avenues of handling tensions may be noted. A number of these children show abnormally dysrhythmic electroencephalographic tracings, usually without evidence of true epileptic patterns, and a certain group may show a high association between enuresis since infancy and firesetting. Stealing, firesetting, vandalism, destruction, aggressive attack, and other antisocial acts may frequently occur, and behavior may shift at times from one form to another or several others; addiction is not infrequent in older children and adolescents. Although their judgment and time concepts are poor, they usually have adequate intelligence and their reality testing in certain areas is quite effective.

Children who have chronic brain damage without emotional deprivation may show a somewhat similar picture, so far as difficulties in impulse controls and judgment are concerned. They usually have adequate capacities for relationships, however, and may show marked guilt with evidence of true conscience formation.

In recording this diagnosis, the specific behavioral manifestations should be drawn from the Symptom List.

2) *Neurotic personality disorder:* These children may show behavior superficially similar to that of the impulse-ridden personality as they act out or discharge tension arising from conflict. They appear, however, to have reached a higher level of personality development, revealing strong influence from earlier repressed neurotic conflicts. Their behavior often assumes a repetitive character, with unconscious symbolic significance to their acts, rather than the predominance of discharge phenomena. Evidence of some conscience formation is manifest from the presence of conflict, accompanied by some apparent anxiety and guilt, the latter leading them at times unconsciously to invite limits or punishment. Impulse controls appear to operate to some extent in the absence of exacerbations of conflict. Their antisocial action, when it occurs, is predominantly a reaction to intensification of conflict rather than the sudden discharge of impulses, as in the impulse-ridden type, or the result of limitations in ego controls, which at times are noted in certain brain-damaged children. Relationships are warmer and more meaningful, although often highly ambivalent. Some overlap with the impulse-ridden disorders of course exists. Many of these children during middle or late adolescence have been referred to as neurotic characters or neurotic criminals. As with the impulse-ridden group, the specific behavioral manifestations should be listed with the use of the Symptom List.

k. Sociosyntonic Personality Disorder

This category includes two subcategories, with some overlap. Children in one group exhibit aggressive, destructive behavior or antisocial personality trends which, though deviant by the larger society's standards, may be consonant with that of the neighborhood group, the gang, or even the family. They should be distinguished from children experiencing developmental or situational crises of later childhood or adolescence, from those with reactive disorders, and from those with other psychopathological disorders outside of personality disorder. Some children in this group can become impulse-ridden or may develop neurotic

personality disorders, although such developments do not appear
to be the rule.

The second subcategory includes personality pictures that
derive from cultures other than that of the majority group.
This would include children in isolated rural settings who may
have repeated hallucinatory experiences, as do others in their
subculture, as well as those who come from societies which
embrace magical voodoo beliefs, among other examples. If
such manifestations or others, like social inhibition when in
strange groups, are only occasional and are not combined with
other personality characteristics and patterns of thought and
perception strongly deviant from the predominant societal patterns, they may be classified as reactive disorders, developmental deviations, or even as healthy responses, with the behavior specified from the Symptom List.

l. Sexual Deviation

Classification in this category should rarely be used in childhood. It should be employed only when the deviation is regarded as the major personality disturbance, with such a degree
of chronicity and pervasiveness in personality functioning as
to dominate the individual's orientation toward social life. Confusion, disturbance, or deviation in heterosexual identifications
and sexually deviant behavior of course may occur in a variety of
pictures and should be classified under the heading of developmental deviation, psychoneurosis, psychosis, or the like. Some
transiently homosexual behavior is known to be characteristic of
many healthy boys and girls in the late preadolescent and early
adolescent years. When actual inversion of heterosexual identification is seen on a relatively fixed basis in middle or late adolescence, and homosexual or other sexually deviant behavior continues steadily, the basic personality picture should be carefully
considered in order to establish clearly the primary diagnosis.
Some alteration in such trends can occur in adolescence and
early adult life, and latent homosexual or other trends can exist
without overt manifestations throughout life.

If the category of sexual deviation is employed as the primary diagnosis, an additional diagnosis of other trends in the personality should also be given where possible, as overly dependent, isolated, etc. The type of sexually deviant behavior should be specified from the Symptom List—for example, voyeuristic behavior, exhibitionistic behavior, panic reaction in homosexual boy, etc.

m. Other Personality Disorder

Under this heading can be placed any personality disorders not considered to fit under other headings, as with so-called cyclothymic personality, where this is felt to be fully developed. As indicated earlier, this category should not be employed for mixed personality disorders.

6. Psychotic Disorders

In childhood, psychotic disorders are characterized by marked, pervasive deviations from the behavior that is expected for the child's age. Psychotic disorder is revealed often by severe and continued impairment of emotional relationships with persons, associated with an aloofness and a tendency toward preoccupation with inanimate objects; loss of speech or failure in its development; disturbances in sensory perception; bizarre or stereotyped behavior and motility patterns; marked resistance to change in environment or routine; outbursts of intense and unpredictable panic; absence of a sense of personal identity; and blunted, uneven or fragmented intellectual development. In some cases, intellectual performance may be adequate or better, with the psychotic disorder confining itself to other areas of personality function.*

Psychotic disorder in childhood is seen as a basic disorder in ego functioning in which the emerging process of ego development shows extreme distortion. This distortion is revealed in

---

* In this general description, the Committee acknowledges its indebtedness to a working group of British child psychiatrists, who have recently established nine points, or criteria, for the diagnosis of childhood psychosis. (See Reference No. 17 of Appendix Bibliography.)

disturbances of those ego functions subserving thought, affect, perception, motility, speech, and individuation. Associated disorders in object relationships and reality testing are also importantly present. Some manifestations of psychotic behavior appear to represent the individual's efforts at restitution or compensation for the psychotic process.

Following the lines of developmental sequence, the diagnosis of psychotic disorder in childhood differs at various developmental levels of expectancy in relation to age. The earliest behavioral manifestations reveal severe disturbances in development of certain basic personality functions concerning the achievement of basic individuation and relatedness to persons. Later stages of development may reveal a failure of integration, a disintegration of the personality, or an arrest in development, with failure to relate to or to test external reality in various spheres. In later childhood and adolescence, severe disturbances may be seen in social relationships, sense of identity, thought processes, and other areas related to ego functioning at these age levels.

In this category are classified children with the general symptomatology noted in the foregoing in whom the ego disorder appears to be the basic problem and in whom there are no pertinent signs of brain damage such as aphasia or other manifestations. Children with chronic brain syndrome or mental retardation may also show psychotic reactions, superimposed upon their underlying difficulty. In such instances the primary diagnosis should be given, and a secondary diagnosis with qualifying phrases indicating the additional presence and type of psychotic disorder.

This category does not include disorders often referred to as prepsychotic, borderline, "with circumscribed interest," latent psychosis or pseudoneurotic. The Committee feels that these disorders are best classified under appropriate subheading in the personality disorders, with specifications as severe and with the manifestations of disturbance in cognitive or particular ego functions drawn from the Symptom List.

The following special categories are recognized as character-istic of childhood. They are presented in order of chronological appearance, since the basis for nosological formulation is pred-icated so heavily upon developmental considerations. Some later-childhood and adolescent psychotic reactions resemble those of adults, but differences related to developmental charac-teristics and other factors should be indicated where possible.

a. Psychoses of Infancy and Early Childhood

1) *Early infantile autism,* considered to be the primary prob-lem, is to be distinguished from the secondary form, in which autism or self-referent behavior follows brain damage or mental retardation. Early infantile autism appears to have its onset during the first few months or the first year of life, with failure on the part of the infant to develop an attachment to the mother figure. The infant remains aloof, showing little apparent aware-ness of human contact, and is preoccupied with inanimate ob-jects. Speech development is delayed or absent; when it appears, speech is not employed appropriately or for purposes of communi-cation. The child shows a strong need for the maintenance of sameness and tends to resist change, responding with marked outbursts of temper or acute and intense anxiety when routines are altered. Sleeping and feeding problems are often severe. Stereotyped motor patterns, often bizarre or primitive in nature, are frequent. Intellectual development may be normal or ad-vanced or it may be restricted and uneven in areas. In any case, the lack of capacity to perceive reality correctly and to communi-cate through speech may render most intellectual functions in-effective.

2) *Interactional psychotic disorder:* This category covers chil-dren with symbiotic psychosis; the group referred to is a wider one, however, embracing other cases with somewhat different features, and symbiotic parent-child relationships may be seen in disorders other than psychoses. Many of these are children who by their histories seem to have developed reasonably adequately for the first year or two of life, with awareness of or attachment

to the mother figure appearing during the first year. Subsequently the child may show unusual dependence upon the mother in the form of an intensification and prolongation of the attachment, apparently failing to master successfully the step of separation and individuation.

In the second to fourth or fifth year, the onset of the psychotic disorder occurs, ordinarily in relation to some real or fantasied threat to the mother-child relationship. The young child often rather suddenly shows intense separation anxiety and clinging, together with regressive manifestations, the latter frequently including the giving up of communicative speech. The picture is usually one of gradual withdrawal, emotional aloofness, autistic behavior, and distorted perception of reality, to a point which may resemble infantile autism. Rarely, the father or another family member may become the interactional partner, as the result of a shift in parental or familial roles. Alternating psychotic pictures in twins are also seen occasionally, beginning in early childhood, as in other interactional patterns.

3) *Other psychosis of infancy and early childhood* is a category for pictures not conforming strongly to that of either early infantile autism or interactional psychosis, although they may show some features of each. It includes children of atypical development who exhibit some autistic behavior and emotional aloofness. Such children may, however, show some strengths in adaptive behavior and assets in personality development. Differentiation must be made from children with developmental lags in cognitive functioning, those with marked depression and apathy, those who may be identifying with a psychotic parent or other person, those with intense anxiety and inhibition leading to the picture of the "frozen" child with action paralysis, or those with other clinical entities.

b. Psychoses of Later Childhood

1) *Schizophreniform psychotic disorder:* This reaction ordinarily is not seen until the age period between six and twelve or thirteen years. Onset may be gradual, neurotic symptoms ap-

pearing first, followed by marked and primitive denial and projection, looseness of association in thought processes, concretistic thinking, low frustration tolerance, hypochondriacal tendencies, and intense temper outbursts. Later developments may include marked withdrawal, intense involvement in fantasy, autistic behavior, emotional aloofness, true disorders in thinking, and a breakdown in reality testing. In other instances, more acute and sudden eruptions at this developmental phase may involve crises accompanied by intense anxiety, uncontrollable phobias, and marked withdrawal leading to autistic behavior and distorted reality testing.

In these children, regression is ordinarily not as marked as in adults. True hallucinations are not commonly recognized until the later school-age period; this may in part be due to the fact that, in the early school-age child, the presence of expected fantasy, some persistence of magical thinking, and an evolving though uneven mastery of difficulties make it difficult to be certain about such phenomena. Bizarre behavior and stereotyped motor patterns, such as whirling, are frequently present. Some children show sudden and wild outbursts of either aggressive or self-mutilating behavior, inappropriate mood swings, and suicidal threats and attempts. Ideas of reference, dissociative phenomena, somatic delusions, catatonic behavior, paranoid thinking, and other manifestations seen in adults may occur. If the psychosis has progressed to the point where intellectual retardation is a central or prominent feature, the clinician may add a secondary diagnosis of mental retardation rather than consider such difficulties as a symptomatic manifestation, since the child's actual intellectual capacities may be difficult to determine.

Crystallization into definite subtypes, as in adults, does not frequently occur in schizophreniform psychosis during this age period, and the prognosis for recovery from the initial episode is generally good. (If such subtypes should be apparent, appropriate classification can be made, using the adult categories.) Many children with this picture exhibit a maturational lag or marked unevenness in motor or cognitive performance; definite signs of somatic pathology in the central nervous system are lacking, although psychoses resembling these may occur in children with brain damage or mental retardation. Children in this category have been most frequently designated as having childhood schizophrenia. The term *schizophreniform* is preferred by the Committee, to indicate the parallels between this disorder and the adult form of schizophrenia, but to emphasize as well the developmental differences and the clinical impression that children with this disorder do not necessarily develop the later form.

Certain children may show continuing mild or intermittent thought disorder without many of the other features described, thus resembling the borderline or so-called pseudoneurotic picture. As suggested earlier, these are probably best classified under the paramount personality heading in the section on personality disorders, with the qualifying statement regarding disturbance in cognitive functions drawn from the Symptom List. The same would hold for the so-called prepsychotic picture with evidence of impending disorganization and decompensation—until the appearance of further changes permits a more definitive diagnosis. Considerations of this kind reflect the Committee's view that all thought disorders are not psychoses, nor are all psychoses schizophrenia.

2) *Other psychosis of later childhood:* Herein may be included psychoses of types other than the preceding, as identified. Psychotic reactions of the schizo-affective type may appear in childhood, but manic-depressive psychoses of a clear-cut nature are only rarely if ever seen. When these are encountered, they can be classified under the heading of *other psychotic disorder,* with a statement regarding cyclic, elated, or depressed behavior drawn from the Symptom List.

c. *Psychoses of Adolescence*

1) *Acute confusional state:* During adolescence and the post-adolescent period a particular type of psychotic disorder may

occur, related to the developmental problems of the stage. The onset is often rather abrupt, with acute and intense anxiety, depressive trends, confusion in thinking, and depersonalization, among other manifestations. Disturbances in the development of a sense of identity are apparent in such persons, but evidence of a true thought disorder or marked breakdown in reality testing is usually lacking. The adolescent can frequently maintain a capacity for meaningful emotional relationships in spite of the disorder, and shows, albeit unevenly, the presence of varying adaptive capacities.

This state should be differentiated from schizophrenic and dissociative reactions, as well as from anxiety, depression, or feelings of depersonalization, which occur in normal adolescents. Overlays of hysterical and other psychoneurotic symptoms may be present; such phenomena should be classified as secondary categories under appropriate headings or included as symptomatic behavior drawn from the Symptom List. The prognosis is generally good for immediate recovery; a deep-seated personality disorder may later be seen to underlie the psychotic picture, however, or it may be related to an acutely decompensating personality disorder. When such prior personality trends can be seen clearly, the type of personality disorder should be specified as an additional diagnosis.

2) *Schizophrenic disorder, adult type:* These disorders resemble adult schizophrenia, although some minor differences may be present that are related to the developmental level. Although many cases are undifferentiated and are often acute, with rapid subsidence, subtypes of simple, catatonic, paranoid, and hebephrenic nature can often be seen on a more chronic or recurrent basis, as in adults.

3) *Other psychosis of adolescence:* This category should be reserved for those disorders which do not fit the preceding categories in adolescence. These may include sweeping regressive pictures of psychotic degree, with associated thought disorders, that do not assume true schizophrenic coloration; transient catatonic states or marked dissociative states may be seen, at times

with strong hysterical features. Although individuals in whom these states occur may have severe underlying personality disorders that should be specified, the prognosis of rapid recovery from such immediate psychotic episodes in this age group may be good; the presence or absence of psychosis alone is not necessarily related to long-term outlook. If, as has been described rarely, manic-depressive pychosis is seen in this age group, the adult diagnosis can be employed and the Symptom List used to describe special behavior referent to this development level.

7. Psychophysiologic Disorders

Following the Standard Nomenclature, this term is used in preference to the term, *psychosomatic disorders,* since the latter refers to an approach to the field of medicine as a whole rather than to certain specified conditions. It is preferred to the term, *somatization reactions,* which implies that these disorders are simply other forms of psychoneurotic disorder.

The term, *psychophysiologic (or vegetative) disorder,* refers to those disorders in which there is a significant interaction between somatic and psychological components, with varying degrees of weighting of each component. Psychophysiologic disorders may be precipitated and perpetuated by psychological or social stimuli of stressful nature. Such disorders ordinarily involve those organ systems that are innervated by the autonomic or involuntary portion of the central nervous system. The symptoms of disturbed functioning at the vegetative level are regarded as having physiological rather than psychological symbolic significance, in contrast to conversion disorders, which involve voluntary innervated structures. Structural change occurs in psychophysiologic disorders, continuing to a point that may be irreversible and that may threaten life in some cases. Such disorders thus do not seem to represent simple physiologic concomitants of emotions, as may occur in psychoneurotic disorders of anxiety type, reactive disorders, or other pictures, including healthy responses. Biologic predisposing factors of genic or inborn nature, developmental psychological determinants with a limited kind of specificity, and current precipitating events of individually stressful significance appear to be among the multiple etiologic contributions to these disorders.

Although conflict situations of particular types may be consistently involved in the predisposition toward and precipitation of these disorders, no type-specific personality profile, parent-child relationship, or family pattern has as yet been associated with individual psychophysiologic disorders. Many similar psychological or psychosocial characteristics may be found in children having other disorders without psychophysiologic disturbances. Psychophysiologic disorders may also involve more than one organ system in sequence, with the occasional occurrence of more than one disorder simultaneously. Psychological factors may be implicated minimally in some disorders, while in others such influences may play a major role, together with somatic factors. Certain psychophysiologic disorders are associated with chronic and/or severe personality disorders of varying types, some even bordering on psychosis, while others may occur in conjunction with milder personality disorders or reactive disorders. Developmental considerations are involved, as in the more global, undifferentiated responses of young infants.

A secondary diagnosis of the type of personality picture seen with the psychophysiologic disorder should be specified. If conversion mechanisms in structures with full or partial voluntary innervation overlap with psychophysiologic mechanisms—as in the vomiting which may occur in adolescents with anorexia nervosa—this should be added as a separate diagnosis, and the particular symptomatic manifestations should be drawn from the Symptom List. As indicated earlier, responses to predominantly somatic illness of acute or chronic nature should be classified as a secondary diagnosis; reactive disorders are frequently though not exclusively seen in reactions to acute illness, and a variety of personality disorders, from overly dependent to overly independent, or other pictures are associated with chronic illness.

In the following list of organ systems, rather arbitrarily divided, which may participate in psychophysiologic disorders, some disorders which appear only in children are listed, in addition to those which may occur in both children and adults.

a. Psychophysiologic Skin Disorder

This category includes certain cases of the following: neurodermatitis; hyperhidrosis; seborrheic dermatitis; psoriasis; certain types of pruritis; certain types of alopecia; certain atopic reactions such as eczema, urticaria, and angioneurotic edema; certain types of verruca vulgaris, herpes simplex, and acne.

b. Psychophysiologic Musculoskeletal Disorder

This category includes certain cases of the following: low back pain; rheumatoid arthritis; "tension" headaches and other myalgias; certain types of muscle cramps; bruxism and certain types of dental malocclusion (both these latter may involve some conversion components).

c. Psychophysiologic Respiratory Disorder

This category includes certain cases of the following: bronchial asthma; allergic rhinitis; certain types of chronic sinusitis; some cases of hiccoughs and breath-holding spells. Hyperventilation syndromes and sighing respirations appear most often to partake of predominantly voluntarily innervated mechanisms and may, if psychodynamic factors indicate, be classified under conversion reactions.

d. Psychophysiologic Cardiovascular Disorder

This category may overlap somewhat with respiratory disorders; it includes certain cases of paroxysmal tachycardia; certain types of peripheral vascular spasm, such as Raynaud's disease and central angiospastic retinopathy; migraine; erythromelalgia; causalgia; vasodepressor (as distinguished from conversion) syncope; certain types of epistaxis; essential hypertension; some cases of hypotension, and, in adolescents and adults, eclampsia.

e. Psychophysiologic Hemic and Lymphatic Disorder

Numerous physiologic concomitants of anxiety are seen in relation to this system, including variations in the blood level of leukocytes, lymphocytes, eosinophiles, glutathione values, relative blood viscosity, clotting time, hematocrit, and sedimentation rate. These ordinarily are reversible; chronic or recurrent states of leukocytosis or lymphocytosis may occur, however, as may alterations in other physiologic values, which may be classified under this heading. Leukemia and lymphoma, as well as some cases of pernicious anemia, apparently may be precipitated by psychologic and interpersonal stimuli; these should be classified under existing headings of predominantly physical disease, with a secondary personality diagnosis, for example, reactive disorder of depressive type.

f. Psychophysiologic Gastrointestinal Disorder

This category includes: certain cases of peptic ulcer; chronic gastritis; ulcerative colitis; cardiospasm; mucous colitis; spastic or irritable colon; certain types of constipation; certain types of nonspecific diarrhea; certain cases of regional enteritis; some types of "heartburn" and gastric hyperacidity; pseudopeptic ulcer syndrome; certain types of pylorospasm; anorexia nervosa; megacolon (nonganglionic type); idiopathic celiac disease and nontropical sprue; certain types of polydypsia; reactive obesity; certain types of marasmus or failure to thrive; persistent colic; certain types of recurrent vomiting without significant symbolic components; certain disorders in salivation, and some types of periodontal disease.

g. Psychophysiologic Genitourinary Disorder

This category includes: certain cases of menstrual disturbances, such as dysmenorrhea, amenorrhea, and premenstrual tension; certain types of functional uterine bleeding; certain types of leukorrhea; certain types of polyuria and dysuria; certain types of vesical paralysis; certain types of urethral and vaginal discharges; and some instances of persistent glycosuria without diabetes. Habitual abortion, male and female infertility, and other disorders may occur in older adolescents and adults. Disturbances in the sexual function of the genital organs in older adolescents (as in vaginismus, frigidity, frequent erections, dyspareunia, priapism) often involve conversion disorders of the voluntarily innervated musculature; certain cases, however, may include psychophysiologic components.

h. Psychophysiologic Endocrine Disorder

This category includes: certain cases of hyperinsulinism; certain types of growth disturbances; and, in adolescents and adults, pseudocyesis and certain disorders in lactation.

i. Psychophysiologic Nervous System Disorder

This category includes certain cases of asthenic disorders, formerly often called neurasthenia, although some may be classified as conversion disorders; idiopathic epilepsy (including petit mal, psychomotor epilepsy, and other equivalents); narcolepsy; certain types of sleep disturbances; spasmus nutans; dizziness; vertigo; certain types of hyperactivity; motion sickness; and certain recurrent fevers.

j. Psychophysiologic Disorders of Organs of Special Sense

This category includes certain cases of glaucoma; asthenopia; keratitis; blepharospasm; Ménière's syndrome; certain types of amblyopia; and certain types of tinnitus and hyperacusis.

k. Other psychophysiologic disorders

Here may be included any disorders which do not fit into the foregoing categories. Certain metabolic disturbances, such as acute intermittent porphyria, may be classified under this heading, as may certain cases of obesity in which metabolic predisposition plays an important role, along with psychologic factors—for example, the developmental type of obesity.

8. Brain Syndromes

These disorders, as indicated in the Standard Nomenclature, are characterized by impairment of orientation, judgment, discrimination, learning, memory, and other cognitive functions, as well as by frequent lability of affect. Such disorders are basically caused by diffuse impairment of brain tissue, particularly that of the cerebral cortex, from any cause. Associated with the basic syndrome, in children as in adults, may be other personality disturbances, such as psychotic manifestations, neurotic manifestations, or disturbances in behavior. These associated disorders are not necessarily related in severity to the degree of the brain tissue dysfunction or to the degree of brain damage. They are determined by predisposing personality patterns, current emotional conflicts, the level of development of the child, and the family interpersonal relationships, as well as by the nature of the precipitating brain disorder and its meaning to child and parents.

As in adults, such associated disorders are often looked upon as having been released by the brain disorder and having been superimposed upon or intertwined with it. In infants and young children, however, later personality development may be influenced by such disorders, whose manifestations may be quite different from those in older children and adults. The young child appears to be able, in marked measure, to compensate during further development for insults to the central nervous system. Certain functions most recently developed may be most vulnerable to such insults, while those developed earlier may be less affected. On the other hand, functions not yet developed may be interfered with, particularly those relating to the cognitive aspects of learning and the development of impulse controls. It is thus much harder in children than in adults to correlate the severity of cognitive difficulty with the severity of the brain pathology. Artificial separations between totally organic and completely functional problems in this area are particularly inappropriate, conceptually and clinically, as indicated earlier in a more general sense.

Children affected by localized rather than diffuse lesions of the brain may react in various ways, dependent only in part on the brain functions which are interfered with. Compensation can often occur to a considerable degree during development. Within broad limits the reactions of the parents and other family members, together with other components of the environment, appear to be the most influential determinants of the way in which the child is able to handle the defect.

To quote the Standard Nomenclature, "The brain syndromes of diffuse nature are separated, with much overlap, into acute and chronic, with regard to differences in prognosis, treatment, and the course of illness. The terms, acute and chronic, refer primarily to the degree of reversibility of brain pathology and the accompanying brain syndrome and not to the etiology or even necessarily the onset or duration of the initial illness or insult to the central nervous system. Since the same etiology may produce either temporary or permanent brain damage, a brain disorder which appears reversible, hence acute, at its beginning, may prove later to have left permanent damage and a persistent brain syndrome, which will then be diagnosed as chronic." This statement applies to children as well as adults. In the discussion to follow, differences in the clinical pictures relevant to childhood will be stressed.

a. Acute Brain Syndromes

Under this heading should be classified those types of acute brain disorders associated with intracranial infection, systemic infection, drug or poison intoxication, alcohol intoxication, trauma, circulatory disturbances, certain types of convulsive disorder, metabolic disturbances, and certain disorders of unknown etiology such as multiple sclerosis.

In general, these disorders in children, as in adults, produce a delirium, involving a disturbance in awareness as the result of the alteration of cerebral metabolism. These pictures may be gross and easily identifiable, characterized by wildly agitated or confused behavior and hallucinatory experiences, the latter arising from misperception of stimuli in the environment. They may also be subclinical, however, with subtle disturbance in awareness or mildly stuporous states, withdrawn behavior, or irrational fears. Perceptual-motor difficulties may persist for some time, even if compete recovery occurs, rendering the child more vulnerable to learning difficulties, upon return to school, in the absence of persistent brain damage.

Preexisting or underlying psychotic, psychoneurotic, or personality disorders may be made more manifest after such insults to the central nervous system, while reactive disorders or later developmental deviations in cognitive or other areas may result from their impact and reverberations. The particular type of reactive disorder or underlying personality disturbance should be specified, with the help of the Symptom List regarding specific symptoms.

b. Chronic Brain Syndromes

These disorders result from "relatively permanent, more or less irreversible, diffuse impairment of cerebral tissue function." Such impairment may occur as the result of congenital cranial anomalies, the cerebral palsies and other disorders arising from prenatal or perinatal damage to the brain, syphilis of the central nervous system, intoxication of various types, brain trauma, convulsive disorder, disturbances of metabolism, growth or nutrition, intracranial neoplasm, or heredodegenerative factors such as Schilder's encephalitis, Heller's disease, etc. Some disturbances in memory, judgment, orientation, comprehension, affect, and learning capacity may persist permanently, accompanied by remarkable compensations at times in individual children during the course of development.

Contrary to earlier impressions, there appears to be no specific type of personality disorder associated in children with all chronic brain syndromes. Rather there appear to be differing personality tendencies, ranging from overly anxious through obsessive-compulsive to overindependent, with frequent developmental lags in personality organization and other developmental deviations.

These psychological factors appear in varying admixtures with the effects upon behavior of the underlying brain damage; for example, some of the psychological features may represent a reaction to the child's perceptions of his own limitations.

One particular syndrome is frequently seen in preschool and young school-age children with cerebral cortical damage of diffuse nature resulting from cerebral insult at birth, in infancy or in very early childhood. This syndrome is frequently but not invariably characterized by hyperactivity, distractibility, and impulsivity, among other features. Diffuse abnormalities are ordinarily present in the electroencephalogram and on electromyography. Difficulties in perceptual-motor functions, spatial orientation, and cerebral integration or organizational capacities, with waxing and waning in effectiveness, are characteristic, leading to problems in employing symbols as, for example, in reading and writing and in abstract concept formation. Specific neurological lesions are rarely demonstrable, and diagnosis must be made on the basis of the history together with the above findings.

Due caution must be employed in making such a diagnosis. Young children with significant psychological disturbance may also exhibit difficulties in impulse control, distractibility, and hyperactivity, together with delayed perceptual-motor development and dysrhythmic electroencephalographic patterns, in the absence of any history or specific signs of brain damage. Thus careful differentiation must be made from reactive disorders or developmental lags or deviations in cerebral integration. Signs of such cerebral dysfunction may not arise from somatic sources alone; therefore, diagnoses of organicity or minimal brain damage, based principally on behavioral manifestations, seem open to much question.

Many children with chronic brain syndromes are not significantly retarded in intellectual development; they often show significant learning difficulties, however, and may function at a mentally retarded level, with psychological and social factors playing a contributory role. If mental retardation is present, this should be specified. A diagnosis should be made in each instance of the predominant personality picture associated with the brain syndrome, as in developmental deviations of affective nature, or personality, psychoneurotic, or psychotic disorders*; individual symptoms can be listed.

9. Mental Retardation

In dealing with this category, the publications, BASIC CONSIDER-ATIONS IN MENTAL RETARDATION: A PRELIMINARY REPORT and MENTAL RETARDATION: A FAMILY CRISIS—THE THERAPEUTIC ROLE OF THE PHYSICIAN (see Appendix),† by the Committee on Mental Retardation of the Group for the Advancement of Psychiatry, should be consulted for a thorough and dynamic discussion of the problems in development and adaptation posed for children and families by this disorder, as well as some of the problems in classification. The Committee on Mental Retardation has drawn upon the existing classifications in this area, including the International Classification, which rely upon existing knowledge of etiologic factors. The Committee concludes that three large groups are involved: *biological, environmental,* and *intermediate.*

The biological group includes conditions with known etiologic factors affecting brain function, such as prenatal infections, toxic influences, and trauma; birth trauma; postnatal trauma; metabolic disturbances; new growths; and congenital abnormalites such as Mongolism, as well as conditions with demonstrable cerebral lesions of unknown etiology, such as demyelinating and hypermyelinating diseases and cerebellar degeneration.

The environmental group includes psychological disturbances, such as severe anxiety or the results of significant emotional deprivation. Sociocultural factors appear also to be involved. These

---

* As this monograph went to press, the Committee was informed that the Committee on Nomenclature and Statistics of the American Psychiatric Association was engaged, together with committees from other nations, in modifying the present Standard Nomenclature to fit more closely with the International Classification. If, as seems likely, the brain syndromes are subdivided into "psychotic" and "nonpsychotic" categories, such designation could be added to the diagnosis as a modifying phrase, or separate subcategories could be introduced for coding purposes.

† Appendix Bibliography references 8 and 9.

range from inadequate emotional and intellectual stimulation in economically and educationally deprived families, to the operation of culture-bound characteristics in tests of intellectual functioning, which appear to penalize children from cultural backgrounds that differ from those prevailing for the children on whom the tests were standardized.

The intermediate group includes mental retardation arising from both biological and environmental factors, such as sensory organ defects, especially auditory, and certain cases of childhood psychosis with apparently strong hereditary constitutional factors interwoven with psychological and interpersonal influences.

As the cited publications and others recognize, environmental factors, including psychological and social or interpersonal forces, are operative to some degree in every child with mental retardation. Thus, assessment of the degree of effectiveness in functioning of the child cannot rest on tests of intellectual capacity alone, given all the known limitations as well as the demonstrated assets of the intelligence quotient. Such assessment must also take into consideration cultural, physical, and emotional determinants, as well as school, vocational and social effectiveness of the child. I' is well known that predictions of later intellectual functioning on the basis of psychological tests in infancy and early childhood have been relatively unreliable. Thus, even in severely damaged children, a diagnosis should never be made on the basis of a single test but should be based on proper follow-up. Such an approach is necessary if one is to allow for the striking changes in intellectual functioning which are known to occur during the course of development in childhood. This is especially true for mentally retarded children, who may show a significant increase in functioning intellectual level up to the limits of their actual capacity as the result of receiving adequate stimulation previously unavailable to them. On the basis of these and related considerations, the term *mental retardation* is preferred in childhood to *mental deficiency,* indicating as it does a more dynamic and expectant approach to diagnosis—except, perhaps, for very seriously damaged children.

The Committee recommends that the Classification of the American Association for Mental Deficiency (see Appendix Bibliography, Reference No. 1) be used for purposes of statistical reporting, with the degree of intellectual functioning specified as borderline mental retardation, mild, moderate, or severe, in accordance with that system. The limitations inherent in an exact numerical score for the IQ of any child should be emphasized, however, and it should be borne in mind that a child near the top of one range may actually be capable of functioning in the lower portion of the next higher range.

Children with mental retardation may show varying personality pictures, some associated with the intellectual limitations and the child's awareness of his defect. Psychotic, neurotic, or personality disorders may occur, as may reactive disorders or specific developmental deviations. The particular personality diagnosis associated with mental retardation should be specified if at all possible. Some children with mild mental retardation in the absence of significant hereditary or somatic factors may be classified under the heading of developmental deviation; such children may be exhibiting a delay in development of particular cognitive functions, or they may fall at the lower end of the distribution curve of intellectual capacities.

10. Other Disorders

This category can be used for any disorders which may be described in the future or for disorders which may eventually be split off from disorders already recognized. It can also be used as a substitute for any one of the other major categories where the individual clinician entertains some reservations about them and still wishes to be able to categorize a child for statistical and research purposes.

4

SYMPTOM LIST

This list of disturbances in behavior of children and adolescents has been prepared for elective usage, as described in Chapter 2 of the report. Thus it is similar in purpose to the List of Supplementary Terms included in Appendix C, MENTAL DISORDERS: DIAGNOSTIC AND STATISTICAL MANUAL, published in 1952 by the American Psychiatric Association. This Symptom List includes those entries from that list which pertain to children and adolescents, as well as many more gathered from textbooks on child psychiatry and other pertinent publications, and from the clinical experience of members of the Committee.

Insofar as possible the symptoms are organized, for convenience in finding, around broad categories related to bodily functions, development, and behavior. No classificatory significance or causal relationships are imputed to this pattern of organization. No attempt has been made to distinguish which among the entries listed are predominantly psychopathological or predominantly neuropathological in origin. Many symptoms may derive from either level or may be mixed in origin. The term *symptom* is here used only in the broadest sense of deviant or disturbed behavior; it is not employed in the symbolic sense as applied earlier to the process of symptom formation, nor is it utilized in the traditional clinical sense of distinction between symptoms and signs. A number of the symptoms may even represent healthy behavior at a particular level of development.

Outline of Symptom List

I. *Disturbances Related to Bodily Functions*
    A. Eating
    B. Sleeping
    C. Bowel Function
    D. Bladder Function
    E. Speech
       1. Absence of Speech
       2. Disorders in Articulation
       3. Disorders in Rhythm
       4. Disorders in Phonation
       5. Disorders in Speech Comprehension
       6. Disorders of Symbolization
       7. Other Speech Disturbances
    F. Motoric Patterns
    G. Rhythmic Patterns
    H. Habit Patterns
    I. Sensory Disturbances
       1. General
       2. Special Senses
    J. Other Disturbances Related to Bodily Functions
       1. Generalized
       2. Localized
       3. Other Bodily Systems
          a. Skin
          b. Musculoskeletal
          c. Respiratory
          d. Cardiovascular
          e. Hemic and Lymphatic
          f. Gastrointestinal
          g. Genitourinary
          h. Endocrine
          i. Nervous System
          j. Organs of Special Sense
II. *Disturbances Related to Cognitive Functions*
    A. Precocity

B. Learning Failure
C. Disturbances in Thinking
D. Disturbances in Memory
E. Disturbances in Awareness
F. Other Cognitive Disturbances

III. *Disturbances in Affective Behavior*
A. Manifestly Fearful Behavior
B. Manifest Anxiety
C. Depressive Symptoms
D. Euphoric Behavior
E. Hypochondriacal Behavior
F. Other Affective States

IV. *Disturbances Related to Development*
A. Physical Growth
B. Maturational Patterns

V. *Disturbances in Social Behavior*
A. Aggressive Behavior
1. Externally Directed
2. Internally Directed
B. Antisocial Behavior
C. Oppositional Behavior
D. Isolating Behavior
E. Problems in Dominance-Submission
F. Problems in Dependence-Independence
1. Overly Dependent Behavior
2. Overly Independent Behavior
G. Problems in Sexual Adjustment

VI. *Difficulties in Integrative Behavior*

VII. *Other Behavioral Disturbances*
A. Stereotyped Behavior
B. Tantrum Behavior
C. Hallucinations
D. Delusions
E. Malingering Behavior
F. Addictive Behavior

VIII. *Other Disturbances Not Elsewhere Listed*

Symptom List

I.   *Disturbances Related to Bodily Functions*
   A. *Eating*
      1. Anorexia
      2. Feeding inhibition
      3. Food fads
      4. Food refusal
      5. Food rituals
      6. Food smearing
      7. Overeating (bulimia, hyperphagia, etc.)
      8. Polydypsia
      9. Refusal to chew
     10. Regurgitation
     11. Sucking difficulties
     12. Weaning difficulties
     13. Other eating difficulties
   B. *Sleeping*
      1. Bedtime rituals
      2. Chronic resistance to sleep
      3. Difficulty in falling asleep
      4. Excessive sleepiness
      5. Fear of the dark
      6. Fitful Sleep
      7. Hypersomnia
      8. Hypnogogic or hypnopompic states
      9. Hyposomnia
     10. Insomnia
     11. Night fears
     12. Night terrors
     13. Nightmares
     14. Somnambulism
     15. Talking in sleep
     16. Unwillingness to sleep alone
     17. Other sleeping difficulties
   C. *Bowel Function*
      1. Anal masturbation

2. Constipation
3. Coprophagia
4. Diarrhea
5. Encopresis (specify continuing or regressive)
6. Excessive flatulence
7. Resistance to training
8. Smearing
9. Toilet rituals
10. Withholding stools
11. Other bowel function difficulties

D. *Bladder Function*
1. Enuresis (specify nocturnal, diurnal, intentional; continuing or regressive)
2. Resistance to training
3. Toilet rituals
4. Urinary frequency
5. Urinary retention
6. Urinary urgency
7. Other bladder function difficulties

E. *Speech*
1. *Absence of Speech*
   a. Aphonia
   b. Elective mutism
   c. Deaf-mutism
   d. Delayed speech
   e. Other forms of speech absence
2. *Disorders in Articulation*
   a. Distortion of sounds
      1) Lisping
      2) Gammacism (difficulty with gutterals)
   b. Elision of sounds
   c. Infantile speech
   d. Insertion of sounds
   e. Omission of sounds
   f. Substitution types
      1) Lalling (l to r difficulties)

2) Burring (difficulty with r's)
g. Other articulation difficulties

3. *Disorders in Rhythm*
   a. Cluttered speech
   b. Hesitant speech
   c. Rapid speech
   d. Repetition of words
   e. Slurring of speech
   f. Stuttering (includes stammering; specify with or without associated movements)
   g. Other rhythm disorders

4. *Disorders in Phonation*
   a. Anarthria (inability to express words or symbols properly)
   b. Change in voice
   c. Dysarthria
   d. Dysphonia (hoarseness, etc.)
   e. High-pitched (falsetto) speech
   f. Monotone
   g. Nasal speech
   h. Whining speech
   i. Other phonation difficulties

5. *Disorders in Speech Comprehension*
   a. Word deafness (sensory aphasia)
   b. Other difficulties in speech comprehension

6. *Disorders of Symbolization*
   a. Irrelevant language
   b. Malapropisms
   c. Metaphoric language
   d. Motor (expressive) aphasia
   e. Other symbolization difficulties

7. *Other Speech Disturbances*
   a. Circumstantial speech
   b. Compulsive talking
   c. Confabulation
   d. Coprolalia

    e. Echolalia
    f. Humming
    g. Idioglossia (idiosyncratic language)
       1) Twin speech
       2) Other forms of idioglossia
    h. Incessant talking
    i. Interjectional speech
    j. Forced laughter
    k. Loud talking
    l. Neologisms
    m. Obscene speech
    n. Paralogia (Ganser syndrome)
    o. Paraphasia
    p. Perseveration
    q. Profane speech
    r. Pronomial reversal
    s. Punning
    t. Rhyming
    u. Whispering
    v. Speech disturbances not elsewhere listed

F. *Motoric Patterns*
    1. Ambidexterity
    2. Apraxia
    3. Astasia-abasia (inability to stand)
    4. Asynergia (ataxia)—difficulty in coordination
    5. Athetoid movements
    6. Automatisms
    7. Blindisms
    8. Bradykinesis
    9. Catalepsy
   10. Cataplexy
   11. Catatonic behavior
   12. Choreiform movements
   13. Choreoathetoid movements
   14. Combined form of abnormal involuntary movements

15. Disturbances of gait
16. Disturbances of posture (cramptocormia, etc.)
17. Dyspraxia
18. Dystonic movements
19. Echokinesis
20. Epileptoid movements
21. Flexibilitas cerea
22. Hemiballismus
23. Hyperkinesis
24. Hypertonicity
25. Hypokinesis
26. Hypotonicity
27. Mannerisms (specify type)
28. Muscular twitching
29. Paralysis (specify monoplegia, diplegia, hemiplegia, paraplegia)
30. Paresis
31. Poor coordination
32. Pronounced startle response
33. Restless behavior
34. Spasmodic movements (specify type, body part)
35. Stereotyped movements
36. Tics
37. Torsion spasms (of pelvic or shoulder girdle)
38. Torticollis
39. Tremors
40. Other abnormal motoric patterns

G. *Rhythmic Patterns*
1. Head banging
2. Head nodding
3. Body rocking
4. Body rolling
5. Whirling
6. Other abnormal rhythmic patterns

H. *Habit Patterns*
1. Aerophagia

2. Biting and chewing (body parts, clothes, etc.)
3. Eructatio nervosa
4. Eyebrow pulling
5. Finger rolling
6. Fingersucking (specify with or without associated displacement of teeth or mandible)
7. Insertion of objects into body orifices
8. Lip biting
9. Lip pulling
10. Lip sucking
11. Masturbation
12. Nail-biting
13. Nodding spasms
14. Nose boring
15. Nose picking
16. Object sucking
17. Pica (specify non-nutritional material ingested)
18. Picking behavior (specify body part, wound or sore, etc.)
19. Pulling behavior (specify body part)
20. Rumination
21. Repetitive hiccoughing
22. Spitting
23. Stroking (objects, body parts)
24. Teeth-grinding
25. Thumb-sucking (specify with or without associated movements; displacement of teeth or mandible)
26. Tongue-swallowing
27. Trichophagia (hair-eating)
28. Trichotillomania (hair-pulling)
29. Other significant habit patterns

I. *Sensory Disturbances*
  1. *General*
    a. Absence of sensation of cold
    b. Absence of sensation of heat

    c. Absence of vibratory sensibility
    d. Acroparesthesia
    e. Anesthesia, conversion type
    f. Decrease of sensation of cold
    g. Decrease of sensation of heat
    h. Hemianalgesia
    i. Hemianesthesia
    j. Hemihypesthesia
    k. Hyperalgesia
    l. Hyperesthesia
    m. Hypesthesia
    n. Increase of sensation of cold or heat
    o. Itching
    p. Pain insensitivity
    q. Paresthesia
    r. Synesthesia
    s. Other sensory disturbances not elsewhere classified

2. *Special Senses*
  a. *Hearing*
    1) Deafness
    2) Hallucinations
    3) Hyperacusis
    4) Pseudodeafness
    5) Selective limitation in hearing
    6) Tinnitus
    7) Other hearing disturbances
  b. *Vision*
    1) Amblyopia
    2) Avoidance of looking
    3) Blindness
    4) Eidetic phenomena
    5) Field disturbances (gun barrel, etc.)
    6) Hallucinations
    7) Optical illusions
    8) Perceptual disorders

      a) Macropsia
      b) Micropsia
   9) Photophobia
  10) Visual agnosia
  11) Other visual disturbances

c. *Smell*
  1) Anosmia (sense of smell absent)
  2) Increased sense of smell
  3) Other disturbances in sense of smell

d. *Taste*
  1) Ageusia (sense of taste absent)
  2) Increased sense of taste
  3) Other disturbances in sense of taste

J. *Other Disturbances Related to Bodily Functions*
  1. *Generalized*
    a. Body-image distortions
    b. Fatiguability
    c. Incoordination
    d. Invalidism
    e. Lethargy
    f. Pain (specify type)
    g. Paralysis (specify type)
    h. Polysurgical addiction
    i. Weakness
    j. Other generalized disturbances related to bodily functions

  2. *Localized*
    a. Headaches
    b. Incoordination (specify body part)
    c. Pain (specify type, body part)
    d. Paralysis (specify type, body part)
    e. Weakness (specify body part)
    f. Other localized disturbances related to bodliy functions

  3. *Other Bodily Systems*
    a. *Skin*
      1) Acne

2) Alopecia (loss of hair)
3) Angioneurotic edema
4) Blushing
5) Eczematoid reactions
6) Erythromelalgia
7) Hyperhidrosis (specify local or general, nocturnal or diurnal)
8) Neurodermatitis
9) Neurotic excoriations
10) Night sweats
11) Pallor
12) Pilomotor disturbances
13) Pruritis
14) Urticaria
15) Other skin disturbances

b. *Musculoskeletal*
1) Atonia
2) Arthralgia
3) Bruxism
4) Coccygodynia
5) Contractures
6) Low back pain
7) Malocclusion
8) Muscular cramps
9) Muscular fasciculations
10) Tension headache
11) Trismus
12) Other musculoskeletal disturbances

c. *Respiratory*
1) Absent sneezing response
2) Asthma
3) Breath-holding spells
4) Bronchial spasm
5) Coughing tics
6) Disturbances in respiratory rhythm
7) Dyspnea (specify as continued or paroxysmal)

8) Hyperventilation (specify with or without tetany)
9) Incoordination of vocal cords
10) Intractable sneezing
11) Nasal discharge
12) Paralysis of larynx
13) Recurrent coughing
14) Recurrent hiccoughing
15) Respiratory tics (specify as barking, coughing, etc.)
16) Rhinitis
17) Sighing respirations
18) Spasm of glottis
19) Other respiratory disturbances

d. *Cardiovascular*
1) Causalgia
2) Chest pain (angina innocens)
3) Epistaxis
4) Hypertension
5) Hypotension
6) Palpitations
7) Paroxysmal auricular tachycardia
8) Peripheral vascular spasm (specify type, body part)
9) Swelling of legs
10) Vasodepressor syncope
11) Other cardiovascular disturbances

e. *Hemic and Lymphatic*
1) Leukocytosis
2) Lymphocytosis
3) Anemia (specify related to feeding refusal, etc.)
4) Other hemic-lymphatic disturbances

f. *Gastrointestinal*
1) Abdominal pain (specific, chronic or recurrent)

2) Absent pharyngeal reflexes
3) Cachexia
4) Colic
5) Constipation
6) Diarrhea
7) Drooling
8) Dysphagia
9) Epigastric distress
10) Eructation
11) Failure to gain weight
12) Halitosis
13) Heartburn
14) Hyperacidity
15) Marasmus (failure to thrive)
16) Nausea (specify morning, chronic, etc.)
17) Obesity
18) Paralysis of uvula
19) Pylorospasm
20) Vomiting (specify as episodic, cyclic, or chronic)
21) Weight loss
22) Other gastrointestinal disturbances

g. *Genitourinary*
1) Abortion
2) Amenorrhea
3) Cessation of menstrual periods
4) Dysmenorrhea
5) Dyspareunia
6) Dysuria
7) Frigidity
8) Glycosuria
9) Impotence
10) Incontinence of urine
11) Inhibition of urination
12) Leukorrhea
13) Metrorrhagia

14) Miscarriage
15) Nocturnal emissions
16) Oligomenorrhea
17) Ovulation pain (mittelschmerz)
18) Pain referrable to female genital organs
19) Pain referrable to male genital organs
20) Polyuria
21) Premenstrual tension
22) Priapism
23) Recurrent erections
24) Retention of urine
25) Urethral discharge
26) Uterine bleeding
27) Vaginal discharge
28) Vaginismus
29) Vesical pain
30) Vesical paralysis
31) Other genitourinary disturbances

h. *Endocrine*
1) Depressed basal metabolism
2) Disorders of lactation (specify type)
3) Elevated basal metabolism
4) Pseudocyesis
5) Retardation in growth
6) Other endocrine disturbances

i. *Nervous System*
1) Comatose state
2) Conversion syncope
3) Delirium
4) Dizziness
5) Glossodynia
6) Headache
7) Motion sickness
8) Narcolepsy
9) Neuralgia (specify type as atypical, facial, etc.)

10) Phantom limb phenomenon
11) Pyrexia (recurrent fever)
12) Seizure phenomena
13) Stupor
14) Syncope
15) Vertigo
16) Other disturbances of the nervous system

j. *Organs of Special Sense*
1) Absent corneal reflexes
2) Accommodative asthenopia
3) Diplopia
4) Eye spasm
   a) Extrinsic muscles (including blepharo-spasm)
   b) Intrinsic muscles
5) Nystagmus
6) Paralysis of ocular muscles
7) Other disturbances of special sense organs

II.   *Disturbances Related to Cognitive Functions*
A. *Precocity*
   1. General
   2. Specific (specify type)
B. *Learning Failure*
   1. *General*
      a. Learning inhibition
      b. Pseudoretardation
      c. Underachievement
      d. Other general learning failures
   2. *Specific*
      a. Arithmetic disability
      b. Reading disability
      c. Spelling disability
      d. Writing disability
      e. Mixed laterality
      f. Other specific learning failures

C. *Disturbances in Thinking*
 1. Associative (thought) disorder (looseness, fluidity of associations; specify as intermittent or chronic)
 2. Concretistic thinking
 3. Disturbance in reality testing
 4. Distractibility (short attention span, difficulties in concentration)
 5. Magical thinking
 6. Persistence of prelogical thought processes
 7. Other thinking disturbances

D. *Disturbances in Memory*
 1. Amnesia
 2. Impairment of recent memory
 3. Other memory disturbances

E. *Disturbances in Awareness*
 1. Comatose state
 2. Confusional state
 3. Delirious state
 4. Depersonalization
 5. Dissociated personality
 6. Fugue state
 7. Ganser syndrome
 8. Pseudodelirious state
 9. Pseudopsychotic state
 10. Stuporous state
 11. Trance state
 12. Twilight states (dream)
 13. Other disturbances in awareness

F. *Other Cognitive Disturbances*
 1. Disturbances in spatial orientation
 2. Overachievement
 3. Cognitive disturbances not elsewhere classified

III. *Disturbances in Affective Behavior*
 A. *Manifestly Fearful Behavior*
 1. Multiple fears

2. Specific fears (specify type)
3. Other fearful behaviors

B. *Manifest Anxiety*
1. Agitated behavior
2. Anxiety attacks
3. Apprehensive behavior
4. Panic states
5. Separation anxiety
6. Stranger anxiety
7. Uncontrollable crying, screaming
8. Other anxiety manifestations

C. *Depressive Symptoms*
1. Depression
   a. Acute
   b. Chronic
2. Other depressive symptoms

D. *Euphoric Behavior*
1. Cyclic behavior
2. Elated behavior
3. Manic behavior
4. Silliness
5. Uncontrollable laughing, giggling, etc.
6. Other euphoric behaviors

E. *Hypochondriacal Behavior*

F. *Other Affective States* (feelings of rage, anger, apathy, oversensitivity, inadequacy, inferiority, guilt, shame, superiority, etc.)

IV. *Disturbances Related to Development*

A. *Physical Growth* (related to effects of psychological factors)
1. Accelerated
2. Retarded (failure to grow or thrive)
3. Uneven
4. Other disturbances in physical growth

B. *Maturational Patterns* (specify area and type)
1. Accelerated
2. Regressive (specify type, as loss of walking, talking, etc.)
3. Lag in cerebral integration
4. Retarded (includes environmental retardation, delayed laterality, hospitalism, etc.)
5. Uneven (includes pseudomature patterns)
6. Other disturbances in maturational pattern

V. *Disturbances in Social Behavior*
  A. *Aggressive Behavior*
    1. *Externally Directed*
      a. Antagonistic behavior
      b. Cruelty
      c. Destructive behavior
      d. Fighting
      e. Homicidal behavior
      f. Physical attacks (hitting, kicking, scratching, biting)
      g. Sadistic behavior
      h. Verbal aggression (threats, etc.)
      i. Other (counterphobic, etc.)
    2. *Internally Directed*
      a. Accident-proneness
      b. Masochistic behavior
      c. Self-destructive behavior
      d. Self-inflicted injury (specify type, method)
      e. Self-mutilation (specify type, method)
      f. Self-punitive behavior
      g. Suicidal gestures (specify type, method, agent)
      h. Suicidal attempts (specify type, method, agent)
      i. Other internally directed aggressive behaviors
  B. *Antisocial Behavior*
    1. Cheating
    2. Firesetting

3. Forgery
4. Lying
5. Stealing (specify at home or outside, in group, etc.)
6. Truancy
7. Vandalism (specify individual or group, leader, etc.)
8. Other antisocial behaviors (individual, gang activity)

C. *Oppositional Behavior*
   1. Disobedience
   2. Marked carelessness
   3. Negativism
   4. Passive-aggressive behavior
      a. Dawdling
      b. Passive resistance
      c. Other passive-aggressive behaviors
   5. Provocative behavior
   6. Quarrelsomeness
   7. Resistance to change
   8. Running away (specify repetitive, overnight, etc.)
   9. Teasing behavior
   10. Other oppositional behaviors

D. *Isolating Behavior*
   1. Autistic behavior
   2. Egocentric behavior
   3. Excessive fantasy
      a. Daydreaming
      b. Imaginary playmates
      c. Other isolating behaviors
   4. Excessive shyness
   5. Hoarding behavior
   6. Inhibited behavior
   7. Narcissistic behavior
   8. Overascetic behavior
   9. Paranoid behavior
   10. Rejecting behavior
   11. Stinginess
   12. Suspiciousness

13. Wandering behavior
14. Withdrawal
15. Other isolating behaviors

E. *Problems in Dominance-Submission*
  1. Boastful behavior
  2. Controlling behavior (specify active or passive)
  3. Manipulative behavior
  4. Overly conforming behavior
  5. Overly dominating behavior
  6. Overly submissive behavior
  7. Rebellious behavior
  8. Rivalrous behavior
  9. Other problems in dominance-submission (suicidal threats, etc.)

F. *Problems in Dependence-Independence*
  1. *Overly Dependent Behavior*
    a. Clinging behavior
    b. Overly demanding behavior
    c. Whining behavior
    d. Other overly dependent behaviors
  2. *Overly Independent Behavior*
    a. Overcompensatory behavior
    b. Overly generous behavior
    c. Overly responsible behavior
    d. Pseudo independent behavior
    e. Other overly independent behaviors

G. *Problems in Sexual Adjustment*
  1. Bestiality
  2. Difficulties in sexual identification (specify type, manifestation)
  3. Excessive exhibitionism
  4. Excessive masturbation or equivalent (specify equivalent)
  5. Excessive sexual curiosity (peeping, exploration, etc.)
  6. Fetishism

7. Homosexuality (specify type, active or passive partner)
8. Overly feminine behavior
9. Overly masculine behavior
10. Overly modest behavior
11. Rape
12. Seductive behavior
13. Sexual promiscuity
14. Voyeurism
15. Other problems in sexual adjustment

VI. *Disturbances in Integrative Behavior*
   A. Impulsive behavior
   B. Incapacity to play
   C. Low anxiety tolerance
   D. Low frustration tolerance
   E. Overuse of adaptive mechanisms
      1. Marked identification with the aggressor
      2. Marked overintellectualization
      3. Marked projection
      4. Marked rationalization
      5. Overstrenuous denial
      6. Overly dramatic play
      7. Other overuse of adaptive mechanisms
   F. Disorganized behavior
   G. *Folie a deux*
   H. Other integrative disturbances

VII. *Other Behavioral Disturbances*
   A. *Stereotyped Behavior*
      1. Compulsive behavior (specify counting, touching, etc.)
      2. Obsessive rumination
      3. Overmeticulous behavior
      4. Perfectionistic behavior
      5. Ritualistic behavior

    6. Other stereotyped behaviors

B. *Tantrum Behavior*

C. *Hallucinations*
    1. Auditory
    2. Gustatory
    3. Olfactory
    4. Tactile
    5. Visual
    6. Other hallucinatory behaviors

D. *Delusions*
    1. Ideas of reference
    2. Somatic
    3. Other delusional behaviors

E. *Malingering Behavior*

F. *Addictive Behavior*
    1. Alcoholism
    2. Gasoline inhalation
    3. Glue-sniffing
    4. Kerosene inhalation
    5. Narcotics (specify agent as heroin, marijuana, mescaline, morphine)
    6. Smoking
    7. Other Addictions

VIII. *Other Disturbances Not Elsewhere Listed*

APPENDIX

Considerations Regarding Dynamic-Genetic Formulation

Reference was made in the body of this report to the importance of a dynamic-genetic formulation, rounding out and deepening the clinical-descriptive diagnostic label, with the latter, however, remaining the only feature currently susceptible to classification. As indicated previously, the principles and special challenges involved in dynamic-genetic formulations are discussed thoroughly in a publication by the Committee on Child Psychiatry entitled THE DIAGNOSTIC PROCESS IN CHILD PSYCHIATRY.[7] The clinician may wish to use the general scheme outlined in that pamphlet or he may already be employing the scheme suggested in MENTAL DISORDERS: DIAGNOSTIC AND STATISTICAL MANUAL, published as a supplement to the Standard Nomenclature by the American Psychiatric Association.[8] In the latter it is recommended that the evaluation incorporate an estimate of:

    a. External precipitating stress,

    b. Premorbid personality and predisposition,

    c. Degree of psychiatric impairment.

Or the clinician may prefer to utilize the Developmental Profile devised by Anna Freud and her colleagues,[6] the approach to the collection and clinical data described by Beller,[4] or one or another of existing formulations, including some which have attempted to systematize parent-child interactions[1, 2, 3] or to erect a system of family diagnosis or typology.[3, 5, 9]

For the reasons already mentioned, the Committee feels that such available developmental and psychosocial categorizations are as yet insufficiently crystallized to permit systematic classification. For the clinician who wishes to include some such evaluation in his dynamic-genetic formulation, however, the following schematic approach is

293

offered in a thoroughly tentative fashion. The categories simply form points of reference around which dictation of a formulation can be organized.

Dynamic-Genetic Formulation: Factors to be considered in data collection and diagnostic evaluation.

1. Individual Personality Characteristics
  a. *Child*
   1) Intellectual capacity
   2) Basic personality structure (if not included in clinical diagnosis)
   3) Central conflictual area or areas; conflict, external or internal
   4) Characteristics of ego functioning
     a) Predominant defensive and adaptive capacities
     b) Reality testing (perceptual capacities, cognitive functions, etc.)
     c) Capacity for object relations with parents, siblings, peers, etc.
     d) Nature of self-concept, self-awareness, self-esteem
     e) Adaptive or integrative capacity (ego strength), including capacity for mastery and synthesis; frustration tolerance, sublimation potential, balance of progressive versus regressive forces
     f) Current developmental level (psychosexual, psychosocial, with reference to genetic level of origin, fixations, regressions, developmental deviations, etc.)
     g) Degree of impairment in capacity for development, play, learning, socialization, etc.
     h) Nature of conscience or superego operations, ego-ideal
   5) Statement re physical health and relationship to psychopathological picture (if not included in clinical diagnosis).
  b. *Parents*
   1) *Mother*
     a) Basic personality structure
     b) Intellectual capacity
     c) Central conflictual areas
     d) Predominant defenses

    e) Capacity for object relationships
    f) Other characteristics of ego functioning
    g) Degree of social or occupational impairment
    h) Statement of physical health
  2) *Father*
     Same as above
  c. *Other Family Members*
    1) Siblings, same as above, plus current developmental level
    2) Others, same as above

2. *Interpersonal Situation*
  a. *Nature of Marital Relationships*
    1) Husband-wife (mutual reciprocity, dominating, parasitic, etc.)
    2) Wife-husband (same considerations)
    3) Interaction of husband and wife as parents (degree of fit, reciprocity, cooperation, complementarity, etc.)
  b. *Nature of Parent-Child Relationships*
    1) Mother-child (supportive, rivalrous, dominating, overprotective, seductive, etc.)
    2) Child-mother (overdependent, hostile-dependent, symbiotic, etc.)
    3) Father-child (same considerations)
    4) Child-father (same considerations)
  c. *Nature of Other Relationships*
    1) Child-sibling (rivalrous, dominating, dependent, parasitic, etc.)
    2) Sibling-child (same considerations)
    3) Child-other (same considerations)
    4) Other-child (same considerations)
  d. *Nature of Intrafamilial Transactions*
    1) Degree of cohesiveness or integration of family unit
    2) Significant subgroup operations (double-bind, triangular, scapegoating, with particular reference to role of child patient)
    3) Equilibrium-disequilibrium balance (leadership, nature of role complementarity)
    4) Degree of external integration of family in community

5) Other characteristics (value orientations, belief systems, etc.)

e. *Nature of Sociocultural Setting*
   1) Social class status and relevant patterns
   2) Ethnic derivation and relevant patterns
   3) Religious affiliation(s)
   4) Occupational status
   5) Educational background

3. *Summary of Developmental-Etiologic Considerations*
   a. *Precipitating Factors:* Nature and degree of reality event or events in relation to impingement upon developmental stage, conscious or unconscious perceptions or misperceptions, etc.
   b. *Predisposing Factors:* Nature of parent-child relationship, family patterns, personality structure, hereditary endowment, biological constitution, integrative capacity, previous events, fixations, chronic physical illness, etc.
   c. *Contributory Factors:* Intercurrent or related physical illness, limitations in mental endowment, illness or depression in another family member, etc.
   d. *Perpetuating Factors:* Secondary gain, use of child by parent as vicarious object, unhealthy or partial solution of conflict through symptomatology by child or parents, family patterns, etc.

Prognostic Statement

Based upon evaluation of the preceding material and upon consideration of other factors emerging during diagnostic study, such as capacity of child and parents to relate constructively to professional staff, their degree of psychological awareness, motivation toward change in significant figures within the family unit, effectiveness of family functioning, etc.

Treatment Plan

Statement of recommendations regarding nature of appropriate therapy (e.g., psychotherapy vs. drug therapy, or combinations, insight-producing vs. supportive or crisis-oriented psychotherapy, individual vs. group or family dimensions, team vs. one therapist, etc.). Also, realistic statement of goals of therapy (symptomatic vs. personality reorganization, degree of possible realignment of family balance, etc.). Special cautions or contraindications to any particular approach.

References

1. Ackerman, N. W., and Belirens, M. L.: "Child and Family Psychopathy: Problems of Correlation," in P. Hoch and J. Zubin, eds., PSYCHOPATHOLOGY OF CHILDHOOD, Grune & Stratton, Inc., New York, 1955.
2. Ausubel, D. P.: THEORY AND PROBLEMS OF EGO DEVELOPMENT, Grune & Stratton, Inc., New York, 1958.
3. Behrens, M., and Goldfarb, W.: "A Study of Patterns of Interaction of Families of Schizophrenic Children in Residential Treatment," American Journal of Orthopsychiatry Vol. 28, 1958, p. 300.
4. Beller, E. K.: CLINICAL PROCESS: A NEW APPROACH TO THE ORGANIZATION AND ASSESSMENT OF CLINICAL DATA, The Free Press of Glencoe, Ill., 1962.
5. Finch. S. M.: FUNDAMENTALS OF CHILD PSYCHIATRY, W. W. Norton & Co., Inc., New York, 1960.
6. Freud, A.: "Assessment of Childhood Disturbances," in PSYCHOANALYTIC STUDY OF THE CHILD, Vol. VII, International Universities Press, Inc., New York, 1962.
7. Group for the Advancement of Psychiatry, Committee on Child Psychiatry: THE DIAGNOSTIC PROCESS IN CHILD PSYCHIATRY, GAP Report No. 38, New York, August, 1957.
8. MENTAL DISORDERS: DIAGNOSTIC AND STATISTICAL MANUAL, American Psychiatric Association, Washington, D. C., 1952.
9. Voiland, A. L., and Associates: FAMILY CASEWORK DIAGNOSIS, Columbia University Press, New York, 1962.

Review of Previous Classifications

1. **Classification by Ackerman: Psychiatric Disorders in Children— Genetic Scheme**
Functional Personality Disorders
Environment
a. Unfavorable environment
1) Physical
2) Social

a) Internal dynamics of family life
b) Interaction of family with environment
b. Favorable environment

Conflict with Environment		Conflict with Self
Habit Disorders Feeding disorders, sucking, biting, vomiting, crying picking, scratching, masturbation, rocking, head-banging, enuresis	*Conduct Disorders* Defiance, rebellion, disobedience, tan-trums, cruelty, destructiveness, hyperactivity, negativism, lying, stealing, precocious sex activity, timidity, withdrawal, asocial behavior	*Neurotic Traits* Jealousy, envy, inhibition of curiosity, play and imagination, inhibition of aggres-sion, sleep disorders, nightmares, night terrors, sleep walking, enuresis, speech dis-orders, masturbation, fears, disturbances of body attitudes; fear of darkness, animals, thunder, water
PRIMARY BEHAVIOR DISORDER		
Structured Patterns of Pathology		
Character Deviations Infantile Isolated, schizoid Inhibited Narcissistic Anxious Hysterical Depressive Compulsive Hypochrondri- acal Paranoid Perverse (psychopathic) Criminal	*Psychoneuroses* Anxiety hysteria (phobia) Conversion hysteria Obsessive- compulsive Hypochondriacal	*Psychoses* Undifferentiated psy-chosis, schizophrenic psychosis (retreat from reality), falsifica-tion of reality, distur-bance of thought, affect, and behavior, vegetative distur-bances, depressive psychosis, manic?
PSYCHOSOMATIC REACTIONS		

Personality Disorders with Organic Base

Body Structure and Function
1. Impaired
   a. CNS disorders
      1) Hereditary
      2) Congenital
      3) Developmental
      4) Degenerative
      5) Traumatic
      6) Inflammatory
      7) Deviant CNS physiology
      8) Endocrine
   b. Physical illness
   c. Body defects
   d. Abnormal body functions
2. Normal

Secondary Behavior Disorders	*Mental Retardation, Structural Type*
Behavior disorders secondary to defect, deformity, illness, deviant physiology, etc.	Weakness of intelligence Poverty of association Perception and apperception impaired Defect of judgment Memory function variable Inadequate motor coordination "Stigmata" of degeneration
Organic Syndrome	*Psychoses*
Cortical impairment Defective organization of intellect, memory, judgment Paucity of association Poor concept formation Limited power of imagination Undue generalization Defective organization of emotions Emotional instability and inadequacy	Psychotic reaction engrafted on organic base Schizophrenic reaction with organic base Undifferentiated psychotic reaction

2. Classification by Beller: Childhood Personality Disorders

a. *Functional Behavior Disorders*

1. *Habit disturbances:* Feeding and training difficulties; auto-erotic manifestations; excessive crying, thumb-sucking, masturbation, scratching, rocking.

2. *Conduct disturbances:* Defiance, negativism, destructiveness, hyperaggression, cruelty, restlessness or overactivity, tantrums.

3. *Preneurotic disturbances:* Inhibition of curiosity, of anger, of aggression; sleep disturbances, night terrors; fear of darkness, of animals, of thunder, etc.

4. *Neurotic disturbances:* Anxiety states, depressions, phobias, conversions, obsessions, compulsions.

5. *Psychosomatic disturbances:* migraine, colitis, ulcers; bronchial asthma; eczema, hives.

6. *Character disturbances* (in early childhood): Multiplicity and pervasiveness of disturbances which are not structured around phase-specific conflicts and which are present on almost every level of development; over or under-intensity and rigidity of reaction from earliest infancy in the expression of physical needs, emotions, and moods, and in reaction to physical and social stimuli.

7. *Borderline disturbances:** Low tolerance of frustration, i.e., responds to slight frustration with uncontrollable impulsivity or withdrawal into fantasy; severe tantrums, with loss of contact; extreme mood swings, very tenuous relationships to people and events.

8. *Psychotic disturbances:* Withdrawal from reality; delusions; inability to identify self and other people; unintelligible and uncommunicative use of language; primary process thinking. Major syndromes—infantile autism, symbiotic psychosis.

b. *Mental Subnormality* (idiocy, imbecility, moronity, borderline subnormality).

c. *Behavior Disorders with an Organic Base* (secondary behavior disorders).

---

* The characteristics described under "character disturbances" above are included under this heading as well.

1. *Etiology:* Hereditary, congenital, traumatic; due to infection, nutritional deficiencies, toxicity.
2. *Somatic pathology:* Neurological disorders; glandular and metabolic disorders; acute and chronic physical illness; physical defects and deformities.
3. *Psychological manifestations:*
   a) *Mental deficiency*—Amaurotic idiocy, Mongolism, cretinism, microcephaly and macrocephaly, hydrocephaly.
   b) *Organic syndromes*—Poorly integrated, erratic, and variable behavior; hyperactivity; distractibility; perseveration; extremes of emotional response, catastrophic reactions to frustrating situations.
   c) *Psychotic disturbances*—Withdrawal from reality, delusions, inability to identify self and other people; unintelligible and uncommunicative use of language; primary process thinking. Major syndromes—infantile autism, symbiotic psychosis.

3. Classification by Brown, Pollock, Potter, and Cohen

Principal Groups
a. Mental Deficiencies
b. Psychoses
c. Psychoneuroses and Neuroses
d. Convulsive Disorders, Including Epilepsy
e. Behavior Disorders with Somatic Disease or Defect
f. Psychopathic Personalities
g. Educational Disabilities
h. Primary Behavior Disorders (i.e., not secondary to other groups of this classification)
i. Social Problems
j. Other Problems

a. *Mental Deficiencies:*
   1) Familial
   2) Mongolian
   3) With developmental cranial anomalies (specify)
   4) With congenital cerebral spastic infantile paraplegia
   5) Postinfectional (specify)
   6) Posttraumatic (specify natal or postnatal)

    7) With epilepsy
    8) With endocrine disorder (specify)
    9) With familial amaurosis
  10) With tuberous sclerosis
  11) With other organic nervous disease (specify)
  12) Undifferentiated
  13) Other forms (specify)
      (Indicate grades of mental level by the term idiot or moron, in each case.)

b. *Psychoses*
    1) With somatic diseases
    2) Manic-depressive
    3) Dementia praecox
    4) With juvenile general paralysis
    5) With epidemic encephalitis
    6) Undifferentiated
    7) Other (specify)

c. *Psychoneuroses and Neuroses*
    1) Hysterical type
    2) Psychasthenic type
    3) Neurasthenic type
    4) Anxiety type
    5) Other

d. *Convulsive Disorders, Including Epilepsy*
    1) Symptomatic
    2) Idiopathic
    3) Other (specify)

e. *Behavior Disorders Associated with Somatic Disease or Defect*
    1) Habit disorders
    2) Personality disorders
    3) Conduct disorders
    4) Neurotic disorders

f. *Psychopathic Personalities*

g. *Educational Disabilities*
    1) Associated with borderline and dull normal intelligence
    2) Special mental disabilities
      a) In writing
      b) In reading

c) In arithmetic

d) Other (specify)

h. *Primary Behavior Disorders* (not secondary to other groups of this classification)

1) Habit disorders
   a) Nail-biting
   b) Thumb-sucking
   c) Enuresis
   d) Masturbation
   e) Tantrums
   f) Other (specify)

2) Personality disorders
   a) Seclusive states
   b) Depressed states
   c) Suicidal threats and attempts
   d) Daydreaming
   e) Excessive introspection
   f) Feelings of inadequacy
   g) Other (specify)

3) Neurotic disorders
   a) Tics and habit spasms
   b) Sleepwalking
   c) Stammering
   d) Overactivity
   e) Fears
   f) Other (specify)

4) Conduct disorders
   a) Truancy
   b) Fighting and quarreling
   c) Disobedience
   d) Untruthfulness
   e) Stealing
   f) Forgery
   g) Setting fires
   h) Destruction of property
   i) Use of alcohol
   j) Use of drugs
   k) Cruelty

      l) Sex offenses

      m) Vagrancy

      n) Other (specify)

  i. *Social Problems*

  j. *Other Problems*

4. Classification by Cameron: Descriptive Code (Profile)

  a. *Developmental*

    Physical handicap or ill health

    1) Physical handicap

    2) Somatic illness

    Intellectual handicapping

    3) Borderline intelligence (IQ 84–69 Binet-Simon or equivalent tests)

    4) Educationally subnormal (IQ 68-53 Binet-Simon or equivalent tests)

    5) Ineducable (IQ less than 53, Binet-Simon or equivalent tests)

    6) Specific intellectual handicap

    Variant of personality type

    7) Deviant toward active, outgoing, aggressive

    8) Deviant toward passive, inhibited, schizoid

    9) Established sexual deviant

    10) Other

  b. *Reactive*

    Primary habit disturbance

    11) Eating

    12) Urinary elimination

    13) Fecal elimination

    14) Sleeping

    Secondary habit disorder

    15) Gratification habits

    16) Tension habits

    17) Disorder of speech

    18) Disturbed personal relations, i.e., jealousy, marked dependency, temper tantrums, etc.

    19) Conduct disorder or delinquency

Motor disturbance
20) Paresis
21) Hyperactivity
22) Tics
23) Other

Education or work disturbance
24) Educational
25) In relation to employment

Individual
26) Psychic symptoms not amounting to psychoneurotic syndrome, i.e., minor fears, phobias, obsessions, etc., as in young children
27) Somatic symptoms of functional origin not amounting to psychosomatic entity, e.g., headaches, stomachaches, etc.

c. *Psychoneurotic Syndrome*
28) Anxiety or phobic state
29) Obsessive-compulsive state
30) Hysterical state
31) Alteration in mood not amounting to psychosis
32) Other

d. *Established Psychosomatic Entity*
33) Asthma
34) Eczema
35) Ulcerative colitis
36) Other

e. *Organic Brain Damage Syndrome*
37) Degenerative
38) Infective
39) Traumatic
40) Toxic

f. *Psychotic Syndrome*
41) Manic or depressive
42) Schizophrenic
43) Toxic exhaustive
44) Other
45) Manifest epileptic attacks of any form

5. Classification by Chess

a. *Normal*
b. *Organic Brain Disturbance*
c. *Reactive Behavior Disorder*
d. *Neurotic Behavior Disorder*
e. *Neurotic Character Disorder*
f. *Neurosis*
g. *Childhood Psychosis and Schizophrenic Adjustment*
h. *Psychopathic Personality*
i. *Mental Retardation*

6. Classification by English and Pearson

Presenting the Psychological Problems of Children as Disturbances of Bodily Areas and Activities

a. *Anxiety States*
   1) Acute diurnal anxiety attacks
   2) Nocturnal anxiety attacks (nightmares)
   3) Chronic anxiety states and phobias
b. *Psychogenic Disturbances of Physiological Functions*
   1) *Disorders of visceral functions*
      a) Disorders of the functions of the upper gastrointestinal tract (oral zone)
         1. Emotional disturbances of alimintation
            a. Chronic anorexia, either general or for specific food
            b. Dysphagia, either partial or complete
            c. Digestive disturbances—the gastric type of conversion hysteria
         2. Reactivation or prolongation of infantile pleasure habits
            a. Finger-sucking
            b. Nail-biting
            c. Compulsion to eat too much food or articles with no food value (pica)
         3. Speech disorders
            a. Inability to speak clearly because:
               1) of organic disturbances in the motor speech mechanisms

2) of organic disturbance in the auditory receptive mechanisms

3) of organic disturbances in the associative sensorimotor speech mechanisms

b. Inability to articulate clearly because of a traumatic speech neurosis

c. Inability to articulate clearly because of stammering, stuttering, or lisping

d. Mutism (delay in learning to talk)

e. Inability to talk understandably because of the use of neologisms

b) Disorders of the functions of the lower gastrointestinal tract (anal zone): Constipation or soiling

c) Disorders of the functions of the urinary tract: Enuresis

2) *Disorders of motor function*

a) Partial or complete limitation of motor function

b) Hyperkinesis

c) Involuntary movements

c. *Disturbances of Social Adaptation*

1) *Aggressive reactions—chronic aggressive states*

a) Stealing

b) Delinquency

1. Occasional delinquency

2. Of feebleminded children

3. Neurotic or due to fear of punishment

4. As psychotic symptom

5. Environmentally conditioned

6. Due to lack of love

2) *Inhibitions of social behavior*

a) Physiological, i.e., limitations of sensory or motor functions

b) Intellectual, i.e., psychic limitations of intellectual functions

1. Limitations of general intelligence

2. Limitations of specific intellectual abilities

c) Social, i.e., limitations of social activities

3) *Sexual perversions*
Voyeurism, exhibitionism, sadism, masturbation and homosexuality

Nocturnal Anxiety Attacks
1) Insomnia—either inability to fall asleep or waking during the night for longer or shorter intervals
2) Sleepwalking and talking
3) Night terrors
4) Nightmares

7. Classification by Gerard

a. *Disturbances in Which Anxiety Is Present in Consciousness*
   1) Chronic anxiety states
   2) Nocturnal anxiety (fear of dark, night terrors)
   3) Phobias
   4) Compulsion neuroses
   5) Depression

b. *Disturbances in Behavior*
   1) Aggressive reactions
      a) Cruelty (retaliation, provocation)
      b) Destructiveness
      c) Stealing
      d) Food refusal
   2) Inhibited reactions
      a) Socially withdrawn
         1. Shyness
         2. Fantasy
      b) Learning inhibitions
   3) Sexual excesses
      a) Masturbation
      b) Peeping
      c) Exhibitionism
      d) Sodomy
      e) Fellatio
   4) Body habits
      a) Thumb-sucking, nail-biting
      b) Nose boring
      c) Picking

5) Enuresis
   a) Diurnal
   b) Nocturnal
6) Soiling

c. *Disturbances in Body Function*
  1) Skeletal muscle involvement
    a) Tics
    b) Stammering
    c) Paralyses
  2) Organ involvement
    a) Anorexia
    b) Vomiting
    c) Bulimia
    d) Constipation, diarrhea
    e) Palpitation

8. Classification by Henderson and Gillespie

a. *Disorders of Personality:* timidity, obstinacy, irritability, sensitiveness, shyness, daydreaming, lack of sociability, emotional disturbances, etc.

b. *Behavior Disorders:* truancy, wandering, temper tantrums, lying, stealing, begging, cruelty, sex misdemeanors, food fads, refusal of foods, etc.

c. *Habit Disorders:* nail-biting, thumb-sucking, incontinence (nocturnal and diurnal), constipation, vomiting, stammering, etc.

d. *Disorders of the So-called Glycopenic Variety:* migraine, crises of collapse, insomnia, night terrors, cyclical vomiting, etc.

e. *Psychoneuroses:* anxiety psychoneuroses, hysteria, phobias, obsessions, compulsions, tics (some).

f. *Psychoses:* schizophrenia, manic-depressive psychoses, etc.

g. *Epilepsy*

h. *Mental Deficiency*—dull and backward group—the result of general or localized defect, e.g., word blindness and word deafness: feeblemindedness, imbecility, idiocy, temperamental defect ("moral imbecility").

i. *Mental Disorders* occurring with, and probably dependent on, some physical disease, e.g., chorea, epidemic encephalitis, trauma.

9. **Classification by Hutt and Gibby (Adapted from Beller's Summary)**

a. *Ego Disturbances*

1) *Transient, Adaptive Problems:* (Habit and conduct problems, associated with deviations in physical growth, physical illness or deficiencies, with mental abilities, and with environmental and cultural stresses and conflicts).

2) *Persistent, Nonadaptive Problems:* (Primary behavior problems, associated with psychological processes or conditions within the child, ranging from trauma, conflict, and fixation to psychosomatic conditions, psychoneuroses, and characterological disorders).

3) *Extreme, Persistent, Nonadaptive Problems:* (Psychoses, including those with affective disturbances, those with schizophrenic solutions, and those associated with organic and neurological conditions).

b. *Constitutional Problems*

(Disturbances presumed to have a somatogenic etiology, including problems associated with specific brain disease, neurological deficiencies or abnormalities, miscellaneous bodily deficiencies, and other constitutional inadequacies).

10. **Classification by Jensen**

a. *Minor Disorders Commonly Encountered in Children*
   1) Problems Associated with Food
   2) Disorders of Sleep
   3) Habitual Manipulations of the Body
   4) Sexual Disorders
   5) Emotional Disorders
   6) Antisocial Behavior
   7) School Problems

b. *Mental Deficiency*

c. *Psychosomatic Disorders*

1) The Central Nervous System
   a) Headache
   b) Migraine
2) The Cardiovascular System
   Fainting
3) The Respiratory System
   a) Breath-holding
   b) Excessive yawning, sighing, or coughing
   c) Asthma
4) The Digestive System
   a) Rumination
   b) Disorders of the bowel
      1. Constipation
      2. Diarrhea
      3. Mucous colitis
      4. Ulcerative colitis
      5. Encopresis
5) Enuresis
6) Muscular System
   a) Tics
   b) Nodding spasms
7) Disorders of the Skin
   a) Eczema
   b) Urticaria
   c) Pruritis ani
d. *The Neuroses*
   1) Anxiety
   2) Phobias
   3) Hysteria
   4) Obsessive-Compulsive States
   5) Hypochondriasis
   6) Anorexia nervosa
e. *The Psychoses of Childhood*
   1) Symptomatic Psychoses
      a) Psychoses associated with infections or toxic disorders
      b) Psychoses associated with convulsive disorders
   2) The Functional Psychoses
      a) Schizophrenia

b) Early infantile autism
c) Manic-depressive psychosis
f. *The Brain-Damaged Child*
g. *Psychopathic Personality*

11. Classification by Kanner

a. *Classification of Psychological Problems of Children*

Adolph Meyer, justly dissatisfied with a psychiatric classification based on the rigid nosological concept of disease entities, prefers to deal with the classification with which one is confronted in psychopathology—"frequently recurring combinations of facts which sometimes occur in pure culture and sometimes in combinations." He does not term them disease entities in the sense of disease of traditional medicine, but he terms them, more modestly, *reaction types* or *reaction sets,* requiring in each case specification of the etiological factors and course.

One of these groups is the anergastic form of reaction patterns—activity denoting actual loss, in the sense of demonstrable focal or diffuse destruction, of cerebral tissue. In the child, the standard types are the disorders attributable to juvenile paresis, brain tumor, meningitis, encephalitis, trauma, birth injuries, congenital anomalies of the central nervous system, amaurotic family idiocy, hydrocephaly, and reactions in the shape of epileptoid responses on the ground of circumscribed or more widespread structural alterations. The postencephalitic behavior disorders constitute an important chapter under the heading of anergastic performance pictures. The connecting link in all these reactions is a deficit, chiefly of memory and judgment, and often of intellectual capacity, in children with structural defects of the central nervous system.

Dysergastic reaction forms—In infectious diseases, intoxications, and nutritional disturbances we may encounter psychiatric problems, usually of a more transient character, appearing mostly in the form of delirious reactions. The outstanding features are hallucinatory episodes, commonly of a fearful or worrisome type, and disorientation or at least misinterpretation of the situation due to haziness or scare. Here we deal with disturbances that are not based on serious structural damage but on temporary remediable affections of the nervous tissues (usually edema) and their metabolic support in fevers or under the influence of poisons or faulty nutrition.

Certain oligergastic reaction forms—There are a number of well-defined clinical syndromes in which mental (and physical) retardation of growth and development is a striking occurrence, but which have no brain pathology. This is true of the cretin and the myxedematous child and of so-called dysgenital imbecility.

This retardation applies in a much more intense degree to the vast number of children with an intelligence level lower than that of the average individual of the same age, yet not low enough to be classed as idiots or imbeciles (exclude anergastic or endocrine possibilities).

Somatic manifestations of personality disorders—A mainly psychiatric "functional" disorder of the child as a whole finds its expression wholly, or more often partly, in a deviation of one form or other of physical functioning, which cannot be identified or correlated with any anatomic-pathological findings. This deviation may appear in the shape of substitutive hysterical paralyses or contractures or anesthesias. In children unusual strain or frustration or unhappiness may find its outward manifestation in headache, vomiting, enuresis, stuttering or twitchings of selected muscle groups. Asthma, eczema, food idiosyncrasies, mucous colitis and spasms of the colon have been proclaimed as the outstanding representatives of this group.

Personality difficulties having a direct relation to non-neurological physical illness—derived from the somatic discomfort from which the child suffers. The child who has myocarditis or pericarditis is often found to be listless and apathetic; children with itching skin affections frequently become irritable and restless.

Personality difficulties having a more indirect relation to physical illness—In another group of children, investigation of their behavior problems reveals a more or less definite relation of the difficulties to previous illness. We find that some of these little patients have developed satisfactorily, have average or superior intelligence, are quite well-adjusted socially, and are members of stable, healthy families. There has been no complaint as to their conduct prior to the onset of reactions attributable to the illness.

12. Classification by Louttit (Adapted from Beller's Summary)

a. *Direct Primary Behavior Problems* (the direct outcome of environmental forces upon the child)

   1) *Problems with limited social significance* (feeding difficulties, elimination problems, sleep disturbances, certain sex problems, nervous habits, etc.)

   2) *Problems with serious social significance*

   3) *Speech difficulties*

b. *Indirect Primary Behavior Problems* (the result of intrapsychic factors and self-related attitudes)

   1) *Actively aggressive behavior*

   2) *Submissive and withdrawing behavior*

      1) Mild disturbances

      2) Severe disturbances

         1. Psychoneuroses

         2. Psychoses

13. Classification by Lowrey

a. *Classification of Psychological Problems of Children*

Group I—Gross Mental Deviations

This group includes the psychoses—ordinarily in mild form —most commonly called prepsychotic; the feebleminded; the epileptic; and, for want of a better place to put them, the behavior disorders following epidemic encephalitis.

Group II—Gross Physical Deviations

This group is highly important because treatment is in considerable part determined by what must and can be done with reference to the physical disability, yet it must help the individual to meet the psychological situation with which he is faced.

Group III—The Neuroses

In the child, as in adults, the neuroses call for intensive and special therapy to stabilize the personality.

Clearly these three groups of problems demand expert treatment and individual attention if much is to be done to alleviate or correct the condition.

Group IV

The complexes and conflicts below the neurotic level represent the common meeting ground of different techniques and the battleground of a variety of professional groups. It shades off on the one side to the neuroses and on the other to emotional disturbances in Group V.

Group V

Presumably the simplest group of problems is that represented by ignorance or faulty training. The lack of knowledge of child psychology or proper training methods results in a variety of difficulties. It is here presumably that child training work and parental education proceed with the greatest profit to everyone. Some difficulties, however, arise not so much from an intellectual problem (even occurring despite the fact that the parent has the knowledge), as from the emotional conflicts of the parents themselves. At this point there is a need to reinforce parental education and child training methods with the type of clinical work which is designed to assist in breaking down those conflicts and complexes which prevent the individual from putting knowledge into effect.

We can, then, say of the first three groups that expert treatment is demanded. In the fourth and fifth groups a variety of techniques come together.

14. Classification by Miller

Classification of the Disorders of Childhood

a. *Subjective disorders*—or such disturbances of mental function as depression, shyness, solitariness, daydreaming, irritability (only felt by the child and not necessarily patent to the observer) overt anxiety, fears or phobias, obsessions, night terrors, compulsive acts, and sleepwalking; intellectual and educational defects, such as general backwardness and special disabilities in reading, writing, and arithmetic (including visual and auditory imperceptions).

b. *Objective disorders*—or disorders of conduct which disturb others in various ways. These include "bad habits," such as masturbation, fidgeting, nose picking, thumb-sucking, nail-biting, and clothes picking; temper tantrums, destructiveness, cruelty, rebellion, and delinquencies, such as lying, stealing, wandering and truancy, sexual offenses against others; and the succumbing to sexual stimulation by others.

c. *Combined subjective and objective disorders*—which have been described as the neurotic accompaniments of behavior disorders and delinquencies.

d. *Mental aberrations*—which may fall into the same nosological groups as are dealt with in adult psychiatry, such as hysterical manifestations, including convulsions, hallucinations, ideas of persecution and other delusions, feelings of unreality and depersonalization, the shut-in personality of dementia praecox, and profound depressions, which fortunately rarely go on to suicide or attempts at suicide.

e. *Sequelae of physical diseases*

f. *Hysteria simulating organic disease*

g. *Other physical handicaps*

h. *Part reactions—*
   1) Respiratory disorders
   2) Cardiac
   3) Gastrointestinal
   4) Urinary: enuresis
   5) Circulatory
   6) Pallor, nausea and faintness
   7) Neuromuscular

15. Classification by Pacella

Classification of Behavior Problems of Children

a. *Organic disturbances* resulting from structural or physiologic alterations of the brain (secondary behavior disorders)
   1) Intellectual inadequacy
   2) Postencephalitic behavior disorders
   3) Posttraumatic behavior disorders

b. *"Functional" disturbances* resulting from reaction to environment
   1) Habit disorders—appearing in the preschool child

2) Neurotic traits, e.g., acute and chronic anxiety states, phobias, compulsions, conversion phenomena, tics, psychosomatic symptoms, etc.

3) Conduct disorders, (deliquent reactions)—chronic aggressive behavior, antisocial behavior

4) Psychoneuroses

5) Psychoses

Mixtures of organic and functional disorders may frequently occur.

16. Classification by Pearson

Classification of Psychological Problems of Children

a. *Disturbances of psychological function,* by brain injury or disease

b. *Disturbances of sociopsychological adjustment,* due to innate or acquired physical differences

1) Differences in brain development (mental deficiency or superiority)

2) Differences in physical development

c. *Disturbances of sociopsychological adjustment,* due to emotional conflicts

1) Anxiety

a) Acute

b) Chronic

2) Psychoneurosis

a) Conversion hysteria

1. Upper gastrointestinal dysfunction

2. Lower gastrointestinal dysfunction

3. Urinary dysfunction

3) Disorders of motor activity

a) General restlessness

b) Convulsive disorders

c) Tics

d) Habit movements, thumb-sucking, etc.

e) Speech dysfunction

1. Stuttering

2. Speech defects

4) Disorders of social behavior

a) Chronic aggressive reactions

    b) Inhibitions of activity
        1. Social relationships
        2. Intellectual activity
           a. General
           b. Specific—reading and other educational difficulties
    5) Psychoses
        a) Reactive depressions
        b) Schizophrenia

17. Classification by Potter

a. *Conditions due to structural damage or defect in brain*
    1) Juvenile paresis
    2) Encephalitis
    3) Mental deficiency
    4) Epilepsy
b. *Conditions due to physiological effect* (probably increasing or decreasing the excitability) of toxic, metabolic, and hormone substances on the central nervous system.
c. *Conditions associated with psychological aspects* of such medical and surgical experiences as physical illness, somatic disability, injuries, and surgical operations; also convalescence.
d. *Conditions associated with environmental situations,* failing to provide for satisfactory ego satisfaction, security or character formation.
e. *Habit problems*
f. *Behavior problems*
g. *Psychoneuroses*

18. Classification by Rickman

Classification of Psychological Problems of Children
a. *Anxiety states* (anxiety neurosis) occur at the earliest in infancy but are commonest at the crises of the vita sexualis, ie., puberty and late adolescence.
b. *Nuerasthenia,* earliest in infancy, commonest in adolescence.
c. *Conversion hysteria,* earliest at the phallic stage, i.e., about three to six.
d. *Anxiety hysteria,* earlier than conversion hysteria, most common after the latency period begins, i.e., about seven years.

e. *Obsessional state,* earliest in childhood, common during the latency period but less common at puberty.

f. *Paranoid reactions,* after the attempted resolution of the conflicts about the parents.

g. *Manic-depressive reactions,* after failure to resolve the conflicts about the parents.

h. *Schizophrenia,* earliest in early infancy, commonest after puberty.

i. *Pathoneuroses,* earliest very early in infancy, not common during the latency period.

19. Classification by Rose

Patterns of Childhood Disturbance:

a. *Developmental Disturbance of the First Year*

   1) *Deviation secondary to conditions of:*

      a) Infectious or metabolic disease,

      b) Prematurity,

      c) Congenital defect with and without surgical remedy.

   2) *Primary tension disturbances:*

      a) Instability and excessive crying (colic),

      b) Sleep pattern disturbance,

      c) Gastrointestinal problem of poor intake, rumination, vomiting, excessive stooling and constipation,

      d) Eczema and nonspecific allergies.

   3) *Primary deprivation syndromes:*

      a) General developmental failure,

      b) Inanition; prone to easy infection,

      c) Monotonous movements,

      d) Apathy and lack of object relation.

b. *Disturbances of 9 to 18 Months:*

   1) Failure of feeding sequence: inability to wean, remaining on liquid foods, anorexia.

   2) Oral tension disturbance: excessive thumb- or hand-sucking; pica.

   3) Failure of muscular sequence: does not stand, crawl, or try to walk.

   4) Failure of social relationship: little smiling, playing, vocalization.

5) Reactions of irritability and withdrawal: rocking, head-banging, aversion to being touched or comforted.
6) Anal tension disturbance: constipation and negativistic withholding, diarrhea and beginning colitis.
7) Respiratory: breath-holding to point of syncope, beginning functional asthma.

c. *Disturbances of 18 Months to 2½ Years.* Relatively minor or unmodified pattern from previous age or regression to such below:
1) Failure to develop in motor behavior, speech.
2) Infantile, irritable behavior, as hyperactive with impulsive movement.
3) Feeding disturbance: selective anorexia, thumb-sucking or pica (lead, paint, hair, industrial toxins).
4) Withdrawal from strangers and from other children.
5) Sleep disturbance, head-banging, self-injury, getting lost, accident proneness.
6) Constipation and unwillingness to be trained.
7) Development of fears.

d. *Major Psychosomatic Conditions:*
1) Milk anemia.
2) Severe asthma or eczema.
3) Severe constipation to encopresis; pseudo-Hirschsprung's disease.
4) Severe ulcerative colitis.

e. *Major Disturbances of Behavior:*
1) Phobic behavior.
2) Psychosis.
3) Ingestion of noxious substances; accident prone.
4) Tantrum behavior to the point of self-injury, i.e., trauma or physiological injury.

Preschool to Beginning School
a. *Regressive Symptoms:* continuation of infantile patterns of eating, elimination, speech and motor behavior, masturbation.
b. *Failure of Maturation:* difficulties with learning patterns, specific speech difficulties, specific reading problem.
c. *Acting-Out and Defiant Behavior Disorders.*
d. *Phobic State*—especially fears of separation, death, injury.
e. *Failure to Develop Give-and-Take Peer Relationships.*

f. *Continuation or Development of General Disturbances* previously cited.

The School Age (6-11 Years)

a. *Regressive or Infantile Symptoms.*

b. *Educational Failure.*

c. *Inability to use Aggression* constructively in maintaining position: fears.

d. Continuation or Beginning of *Previously Listed Severe Disorders* (few psychoses develop at this time).

e. *Acting-Out Disorders.*

f. *Obsessive and Phobic Patterns* (viz., school phobias).

g. *Conversion Hysteria* (rare).

The Age of Puberty and Adolescence (11 to 16 Years)

a. *Continuation or Exacerbation* of new development of previously described symptoms.

b. *Specific Sexual Conflicts.*

c. *Social Conflict in Peer Relationships.*

d. *Major Delinquent Conflicts.*

e. *Adult-Type Psychosis.*

20. Classification by Ross

A Classification in Child Psychiatry

a. *Maladaptive reactions secondary to gross environmental stress:*
   1) Brief
   2) Prolonged

b. *Maladaptive reactions secondary to cerebral maldevelopment or injury:*
   1) Uniform defective mentation (the mentally subnormal child)
   2) Selective defective mentation (the brain-injured child)

c. *Maladaptive reactions secondary to unconstructive interaction between the child and his emotional environment:*
   1) The unorganized child
   2) The negatively organized child
   3) The striving decompensated child (Subgroup: the striving decompensated child with a primary defective self-image)

d. *Psychotic reactions*

e. *Absence of emotional maldevelopment*

21. Classification by Selbach

Mental Disorders in Children and Adolescents

a. *Mental Deficiency*
   1) Simple inherited
b. *Acquired Defects*
   2) Partial disabilities
   3) Other forms of acquired deficiency
c. *Special Forms of Mental Deficiency*
   4) In hereditary organic nervous diseases
   5) In endocrine diseases
   6) Mongolism
d. *Developmental and Sensory Defects*
   7) General disorders of development
   8) Speech disorders
   9) Sensory defects
e. *Psychopathies, Abnormal Reactions (Neuroses)*
   10) Irritable psychopath
   11) Overanxious psychopath
   12) Oversensitive psychopath
   13) Overexcitable psychopath
   14) Affectless psychopath
   15) Unstable psychopath
   16) Self-assertive psychopath
   17) Depressive psychopath
   18) Obsessional psychopath
   19) Others
f. *Neuroses*
   20) Neuropathics
   21) Stammerers
   22) Enuretics
   23) Wanderers
g. *Childhood Psychoses*
   24) Schizophrenia
   25) Manic-depressive illness
   26) Symptomatic psychoses
h. *Asociality*
   27) Asocial, delinquent

22. Classification by Settlage:

Categories of Psychologic Disorders
a. Developmental
b. Situational
c. Neurotic
d. Neurotic character
e. Psychotic character
f. Psychotic
g. Psychologic disorders associated with organic brain damage

23. Classification by Strecker and Ebaugh

Classification of Psychological Problems of Children
a. *Reactive* (70%)
   1) Habit training
   2) Protest and negativism
   3) Recessive (overdependence)
b. *Toxic, Physical and Organic* (20%)
   1) Acute infections
   2) Chorea
   3) Micturition
   4) Organic infections
   5) Endocrine
c. *Mental Deficiency*
d. *Psychoses*

24. Van Ophuijsen

Bibliography*

1. Ackerman, N. W.: "Psychiatric Disorders in Children—Diagnosis and Etiology in Our Time," in P. M. Hoch and J. Zubin, eds., CURRENT PROBLEMS IN PSYCHIATRIC DIAGNOSIS, Grune & Stratton, Inc., New York, 1953.
2. Beller, E. K.: CLINICAL PROCESS: A NEW APPROACH TO THE ORGANIZATION AND ASSESSMENT OF CLINICAL DATA, The Free Press of Glencoe, Ill., 1962.

---

* This bibliography, which is given in alphabetical order of authorship, might well have been shown in ascending order of publication year to emphasize chronology, and the reader is asked to make note of this significant factor when reviewing the recommended titles for detailed reference.

3. Brown, S.; Pollock, H.: Potter, H. W.; and Cohen, D. W.: OUT-LINE FOR PSYCHIATRIC CLASSIFICATION OF PROBLEM CHILDREN, rev. ed., State Hospital Press, Utica, New York, 1937.

4. Cameron, K.: "Diagnostic Categories in Child Psychiatry," *British Journal of Medicine and Psychology*, Vol. 28 (Part 1), 1955, pp. 67-71.

5. Chess, S.: AN INTRODUCTION TO CHILD PSYCHIATRY, Grune & Stratton, Inc., New York, 1959.

6. English, O. S., and Pearson, G. H. J.: COMMON NEUROSES OF CHILDREN AND ADULTS, W. W. Norton & Co., Inc., New York, 1937.

7. Gerard, M.: "Psychological Disorders in Childhood," in E. Harms, ed., HANDBOOK OF CHILD GUIDANCE, Child Care Publications, New York, 1947.

8. Henderson, D. K., and Gillespie, R. D.: A TEXTBOOK OF PSYCHIATRY, 3rd ed., Oxford University Press, Ltd., London, 1932.

9. Hutt, M. L., and Gibby, R. G.: PATTERNS OF ABNORMAL BEHAVIOR, Allyn & Bacon, Inc., Boston, 1957.

10. Jensen, R. A.: "Child Psychiatry," in I. McQuarrie and V. C. Kelly, eds., BRENNEMAN'S PRACTICE OF PEDIATRICS, W. F. Prior, Inc., Hagerstown, Md., 1959.

11. Kanner, L.: CHILD PSYCHIATRY, Charles C Thomas, Springfield, Ill., 1935.

12. Louttit, C. M.: CLINICAL PSYCHOLOGY OF CHILDREN'S BEHAVIOR PROBLEMS, rev. ed., Harper & Brothers, New York, 1947.

13. Lowrey, L. G.: "Some Principles in the Treatment of Behavior Problems in Children," *Journal of Nervous and Mental Disease*, Vol. 73, Jan. 1931, pp. 62-65.

14. Miller, E.: "Classification of the Disorders of Childhood," in Sir Humphrey Rolleston, ed., BRITISH ENCYCLOPEDIA OF MEDICAL PRACTICE, Butterworth and Co., Ltd., London, 1936.

15. Pacella, B. L.: BEHAVIOR PROBLEMS IN CHILDREN. THE MEDICAL CLINICS OF NORTH AMERICA, W. B. Saunders Co., Philadelphia, May 1948.

16. Pearson, G. H. J.: "Classification of Psychological Problems of Children, " in H. A. Christian, ed., THE OXFORD MEDICINE, VOL. 7, PSYCHIATRY FOR PRACTITIONERS, Oxford University Press, New York 1920.

17. Potter, H. W.: Mimeographed outline given to medical students, College of Physicians and Surgeons, Columbia University, 1934.
18. Rickman, J., cited by B. Pacella, *op cit.*
19. Rose, J. A.: "The Emotional Problems of Children," in PSYCHIATRY FOR THE GENERAL PRACTITIONER, abstract from the Seminar Series, The Carrier Clinic, Philadelphia Mental Health Educational Unit of Smith, Kline and French Laboratories, 1958.
20. Ross, D. C.: A CLASSIFICATION IN CHILD PSYCHIATRY, privately printed at 4951 McKean Avenue, Philadelphia, Copyright 1964.
21. Selbach, H.: Cited by E. Stengel in CLASSIFICATION OF MENTAL DISORDERS, *Bulletin of the World Health Organization,* Vol. 21, 1960, pp. 601-663.
22. Settlage, C. F.: "Psychologic Disorders," in W. E. Nelson, ed. TEXTBOOK OF PEDIATRICS, 8th ed., W. B. Saunders Co., Philadelphia, 1964.
23. Strecker, E. A., and Ebaugh, F. G.: PRACTICAL CLINICAL PSYCHIATRY FOR STUDENTS AND PRACTITIONERS, 3rd ed., The Blakiston Co., Philadelphia, 1931.
24. Van Ophuijsen, J. H. W.: "Primary Conduct Disorders: Their Diagnosis and Treatment," in N. D. C. Lewis and B. L. Pacella, eds., MODERN TRENDS IN CHILD PSYCHIATRY, International Universities Press, Inc., New York, 1945.

The authors listed in this bibliography, with the exception of Van Ophuijsen, have offered formal classifications attempting to deal with the totality of psychopathological problems in the childhood and adolescent age range, and their classifications are reproduced in full in the preceding section. Van Ophuijsen's name was included in the list because, although he himself offered in writing only a partial classification, his influence was of vital stimulation to several other authors included in the list. The Committee apologizes if it has missed any major classification, particularly in the European literature.

In addition to those workers presenting full classifications, a number of others have put forward significant typologies or partial classifications or have written cogently about the problems of classification or related matters. Although no such list can be complete, a representative sample of such writings follows. This list is confined to references dealing with psychopathology in the child. References pertinent to the problems of classification of parent-child relationships and family transactions have been listed previously at the end of the section on

Psychosocial Considerations (page 204) and following the section on *Dynamic-Genetic Formulation* at the beginning of the *Appendix* (page 297). Several references referred to in the body of the classification are also included in this list.

Appendix Bibliography

1. "A Manual on Terminology and Classification in Mental Retardadation," prepared by R. Heber: Monograph Supplement, *American Journal of Mental Deficiency*, Vol. 64, No. 2, Sept. 1959.
2. Ackerson, F.: CHILDREN'S BEHAVIOR PROBLEMS, University of Chicago Press, Chicago, 1931.
3. Bahn, A. K.; Chandler, C. A.; and Eisenberg, L.: "Diagnostic and Demographic Characteristics of Patients Seen in Outpatient Psychiatric Clinics for an Entire State (Maryland): Implications for the Psychiatrist and the Mental Health Program Planner," *American Journal of Psychiatry*, Vol. 117, 1961, p. 769.
4. Billings, E. G.: A HANDBOOK OF ELEMENTARY PSYCHOBIOLOGY AND PSYCHIATRY, The Macmillan Co., Inc., New York, 1939.
5. Cheney, C. O.: OUTLINES FOR PSYCHIATRIC EXAMINATIONS, State Hospital Press, Utica, New York, 1938.
6. Dreyer, R. M.: "A Progress Report on a Factor Analytic Approach to Classification in Child Psychiatry," in DIAGNOSTIC CLASSIFICATION IN CHILD PSYCHIATRY, American Psychiatric Association, Washington, D. C., 1964.
7. Fish, B., and Shapiro, T.: "A Descriptive Typology of Children's Psychiatric Disorders: II. A Behavioral Classification," in R. Jenkins and J. Cole, eds., DIAGNOSTIC CLASSIFICATION IN CHILD PSYCHIATRY, Psychiatric Report No. 18, American Psychiatric Association, Washington, D. C., 1964.
8. Group for the Advancement of Psychiatry, Committee on Mental Retardation: BASIC CONSIDERATIONS IN MENTAL RETARDATION: A PRELIMINARY REPORT, GAP Report No. *43*. New York, December, 1959.
9. _____: MENTAL RETARDATION: A FAMILY CRISIS—THE THERAPEUTIC ROLE OF THE PHYSICIAN, GAP Report No. *56*. New York, December, 1963.
10. Jenkins, R. L., and Cole, J. O., eds.: DIAGNOSTIC CLASSIFICATION IN CHILD PSYCHIATRY, Psychiatric Research Report No. 18, American Psychiatric Association, Washington, D. C., 1964.

11. Jenkins, R., and Glickman, S.: "Common Syndromes in Child Psychiatry. I. Deviant Behavior Traits," *American Journal of Orthopsychiatry,* Vol. 16, 1946, p. 244.

12. Krasnogorski, N. I.: "Physiology of Cortical Activity in Children as a New Subject for Pediatric Investigation," *American Journal of Diseases of Children,* Vol. 43, 1933, p. 473.

13. Paynter, R. H., and Blanchard, P.: A STUDY OF EDUCATIONAL ACHIEVEMENT OF PROBLEM CHILDREN, The Commonwealth Fund, New York, 1929.

14. "Psychoanalytic Contributions to the Nosology of Childhood Psychic Disorders," a report by P. Neubauer summarizing papers given by M. Friend, P. Neubauer, C. Settlage, I. Kaufman, and R. Lourie: *Journal of the American Psychoanalytic Association,* Vol. 11, 1963, p. 595.

15. Robinson, J. F.; Viale, L. J.; and Nitsche, C. J.: "Behavioral Categories of Childhood," *Amercan Journal of Psychiatry,* Vol. 117, 1961, p. 806.

16. Sandler, J.; Kawenoka, M.; Neurath, L.; Rosenblatt, B.; Schnurmann, A.; and Sigal, J.: "The Classification of Super-Ego Material in the Hampstead Index," in THE PSYCHOANALYTIC STUDY OF THE CHILD, Vol. XVII, International Universities Press, Inc., New York, 1962.

17. "Schizophrenic Syndrome in Childhood: Progress Report (April 1961) of a Working Party," *British Medical Journal,* Vol. 2, 1961, p. 889.

18. Taffel, C., Miller, K. S., and Flemming, E. L.: "Behavioral Classification Project," *Journal of Consulting Psychology,* Vol. 28, 1964, p. 1.

Since the present communication is not meant to be a textbook of child psychiatry, it is impossible to offer a bibliography covering all or even part of the work of others which the Committee has drawn upon, in addition to the clinical experience of its members, in putting together its descriptions of healthy and pathologic clinical categories in the proposed classification itself. Instead, the following list of the current textbooks on child psychiatry is presented, together with the single comprehensive bibliography in the field available today. Most of the pertinent references dealing with the psychopathology of childhood can be found in these sources.

Bibliography

Berlin, I. N.: BIBLIOGRAPHY OF CHILD PSYCHIATRY, WITH A SELECTED LIST OF FILMS, Psychiatric Bibliographies No. 1, American Psychiatric Association, Washington, D.C., 1963.

Chess, S.: AN INTRODUCTION TO CHILD PSYCHIATRY, Grune & Stratton, Inc., New York, 1959.

Finch, S. M.: FUNDAMENTALS OF CHILD PSYCHIATRY, W. W. Norton & Co., Inc., New York, 1960.

Howells, J. G.: MODERN PERSPECTIVES IN CHILD PSYCHIATRY, Oliver & Boyd, Ltd., Edinburgh and London, 1965.

Kanner, L.: CHILD PSYCHIATRY, 3rd. ed., Charles C Thomas, Springfield, Ill., 1957.

Soddy, K.: CLINICAL CHILD PSYCHIATRY, Balliere, Tindall and Cox, London, 1960.

Although as indicated earlier, the Committee has avoided the inclusion of eponymic disorders and specific syndromes on conceptual grounds, the contributions of many writers have influenced its selection of nosological terms. Only two psychopathological pictures have been included using the terminology of the persons who originally described them. These are *early infantile autism,* described by Leo Kanner, and *acute confusional state,* described by Helen Carlson; they were included as such because of the essentially descriptive character of the terminology employed. The term *developmental crisis,* under the category of healthy responses, was drawn from Erikson's works for the same reason, although other writers have also used the term. A few additional terms, such as *impulse-ridden personality disorder* and *neurotic personality disorder,* have been included for reasons mentioned; such terms have stemmed from particular schools of thought and it is impossible to give credit to the individual who originally employed them.

Other terms, such as *symbiotic psychosis,* employed by Margaret Mahler, *childhood schizophrenia,* emphasized by Lauretta Bender, and *atypical development,* used by Beata Rank, have not been employed as such for reasons explained in the body of the classification, although the concepts developed by these writers and the clinical pictures described by them have been importantly influential in the thinking of the Committee.

In addition to these writers, de la Tourette, Heller, Schilder, Bakwin, Levy, Spitz, and others have described specific syndromes which, for reasons indicated, have been placed under more general headings in the proposed classification. Other writers whose concepts have been drawn upon in the classification have been referred to in the selected references in earlier sections of the report. In the absence of a complete bibliography it is impossible to do justice to the numerous other writers who have made significant contributions of descriptive or diagnostic nature that have been of value to the work of the Committee. These include Aichhorn, Aldrich, Alexander, Allen, Beck, Benjamin, Bettelheim, Blau, Bornstein, Bowlby, Bronner, Bruch, Clothier, Creak, Crothers, Despert, G. Frankl, Friedlander, Gardner, Gerard, Healey, Jensen, and Jessner, as well as Lippmann, Liss, J. K. Menninger, Michaels, Mohr, Orton, Pavenstedt, Redl, Richmond, Roudinesco, Senn, Sperling, Spock, Szurek, E. Taylor, Van Krevelen, Waldfogel, Washburn, and many, many others, who deserve important mention.

Finally, the original sources of many conceptual trends which are influential in the modern approach to diagnosis and classification are exceedingly difficult to identify with any exactness. The interplay of ideas between teacher and student, the cross-fertilization of clinical concepts by those from experimental and other fields of endeavor, and the interchange of written and spoken thoughts among clinicians from various disciplines today tend to shape, alter, and enrich any individual contribution, adding to our present store of knowledge to produce the classifications of tomorrow.

PARTIAL GLOSSARY OF TERMS

affect: Essentially a synonym for an emotion or feeling state, with its subjective mental content, with concomitant physiologic changes and bodily sensations, and with behavioral expressions often of communicative significance to others.

ambivalence: The coexistence of opposing emotions or wishes that may be conscious or unconscious in nature.

autistic behavior: A state of preoccupation with one's own thoughts or fantasies, ranging from temporary self-revery, in healthy persons, to completely self-referent thinking and behavior without regard for external reality.

autoerotic: Pleasure generated within the self; such may be genital, as in masturbation, or derived from thumb-sucking, rocking, or other rhythmic activities that may later acquire a sexual connotation.

cognition: The set of mental processes by which knowledge is gained or integrated or problems are solved; such processes are based on sensory perception and include discrimination, judgment, remembering, conceiving, and reasoning.

conscious: A theoretical construct used to refer to a mental structure or system; also used to refer to perceptions, thoughts, memories, feelings, or sensations of which the individual is fully aware (some may be "preconscious" or available to conscious recall under certain circumstances).

defense mechanisms: Unconscious and automatic adaptive devices by which the ego protects itself against marked anxiety aroused by unacceptable thoughts or feelings. Repression or exclusion from awareness is a major defense; denial of unpleasant reality is frequently seen in childhood; rationalization, projection onto others of unacceptable

330

feelings, and displacement of these onto other situations are among numerous others.

dynamic: Involving the interaction and concentration of forces within the mental apparatus; the concept of conflict is central, between the child's impulses and outer reality (external conflict) or between opposing intrapsychic feelings (internal conflict).

ego: A theoretical construct used to refer to one of the psychic structures or systems within the mental apparatus; the "executive" portion of the personality, which perceives, discriminates, and integrates stimuli from the external world and from within. The ego employs thought processes, communication, defenses, tension-regulation, and other devices in achieving adaptation to reality.

epigenesis: The emergence during the individual's development of characteristics or capacities not present in earlier stages.

fixation: The persistence of earlier patterns of function or behavior; conceived of as representing a pathological response to overfrustration or a clinging to unhealthy gratification.

genetic: Relating to the earlier level of development at which conflicts or problems originated (used in a broader sense than *hereditary* or *genic*).

identification: A complex process, largely unconscious, involving the copying of a model or, at times, certain characteristics of a model whom the child admires.

identity: Awareness of the self as an integrated, whole person possessing certain enduring characteristics and a certain uniqueness of personality.

individuation: The emerging processes of awareness by the child of the differentiation between himself and others, earliest the mother.

intrapsychic: Refers to thoughts, feelings, or sensations taking place within the psyche or mental apparatus, in one of its several structures or systems, at conscious, preconscious, or unconscious levels.

mental apparatus: A theoretical construct used to refer to the combination of several psychic structures or systems; the source of the drives (id), the ego, and the superego.

object relation: The relationship between the child and a loved (human) object.

reality testing: The perception and judgment of external reality events as distinguished from internal (intrapsychic) thoughts or fantasies.

regression: The returning to previously established levels of function or behavior; conceived of either as an adaptive maneuver, permitting regrouping of forces for a future return to higher levels, or as an adaptive breakdown in the face of overwhelming stress.

repression: The automatic blocking or removal from conscious awareness of unacceptable thoughts, memories, or feelings; a central defense mechanism.

role function: The expected behavior of an individual in a group, influenced also by his own characteristics and capacities. Role conflict may occur when an individual is expected to play two roles that are not easily compatible.

sublimation: The unconscious handling by the ego of primitive drives through their channelization into socially acceptable outlets.

superego: A theoretical construct used to refer to one of the psychic structures or systems within the mental apparatus; that part developed by incorporating the standards of the parents and society as perceived by the ego. The "conscience" represents the conscious portion of the superego, although unconscious prohibitions and ideals are also operative.

suppression: The conscious exclusion from awareness of unacceptable memories, thoughts, or feelings.

syntonic: In balance or harmony.

thought disorder: A breakdown in rational cognitive processes in which logical associations are disrupted and primitive fantasy or magical thinking predominates.

transaction: The reciprocal interaction or mutual interaction between two or more individuals or systems involving simultaneous stimulation and response, in contrast to a back-and-forth interaction or stimulus-response situation.

unconscious: A theoretical construct used to refer to a mental structure or system; part of a system of constructs (conscious, preconscious, unconscious); also used to refer to memories, thoughts, or feelings that are not present in conscious awareness and are not subject to conscious recall.

INDEX

338   PSYCHOPATHOLOGICAL DISORDERS IN CHILDHOOD

Increase of sensation of, cold or heat,
    279
  smell, taste, *280*
independent, behavior, Overly, *290*
  personality, Overly, 243-244
Individual   personality   characteristics,
    294-295
Infantile, autism, Early, 253
  speech, *274*
inferiority, *287*
Inhibited behavior, *289*
  personality, Overly, 242-243
Inhibition of urination, *283*
injury, Self-inflicted, *288*
Insertion of, objects into body orifices,
    278
  sounds, *274*
Insomnia, *273*
*Integration and Conflict in Family Be-
    havior*, 201
integrative behavior, Disturbances in, *291*
integrative development, Deviations in,
    229
Interactional psychotic disorder, 253-254
Interactions, family, 200-203
Interjectional speech, *276*
intermediate group, Mental retardation,
    268-269
internalization (conflict), 190
Internally directed aggressive behavior,
    288
*International Statistical Classification of
    Diseases, Injuries and Causes of
    Death*, 176, 267
Interpersonal situation (factor in diag-
    nostic evaluation), 295-296
Intractable sneezing, *282*
Introduction, 173-174
Invalidism, *280*
involuntary movements, Combined form
  of abnormal, *276*
Irrelevant language, *275*
Isolated personality, 244-245
Isolating behavior, *289*
Itching, *279*

J

Jensen, R. A., 329
  Classification by, 310-312
Jessner, L., 329

K

Kanner, Leo, 328
  Classification by, 312-314
Kerosene inhalation, *292*

L

lack of mothering, 188
lactation, Disorders of, *284*
Lag in cerebral integration, *288*
Lalling, *274*
larynx, Paralysis of, *282*
laterality, Mixed, *285*
laughing, giggling, Uncontrollable, *287*
laughter, Forced, *276*
Learning failure, *285*
Lethargy, *280*
Leukocytosis, *282*
Leukorrhea, *283*
Levy, D. M., 329
Lip biting, pulling, sucking, *278*
Lippmann, 329
Lisping, *274*
Liss, 329
Loud talking, *276*
Louttit, C. M., classification by, 314
Low, anxiety tolerance, *291*
  back pain, *281*
  frustration tolerance, *291*
Lowrey, L. G., classification by, 314-315
Lying, *289*
Lymphocytosis, *282*

M

Macropsia, *280*
Magical thinking, *286*
Mahler, Margaret, 328
Malapropisms, *275*
Malingering behavior, *292*
Malocclusion, *281*
Manic behavior, *287*
Manifest anxiety, *287*
Manifestly fearful behavior, *286*
Manipulative behavior, *290*
Mannerisms, *277*
Marasmus, *283*
masculine behavior, Overly, *291*
Masochistic behavior, *288*
Masturbation, *278*
  Anal, *273*
  Excessive, *290*

Acknowledgments

The program of the Group for the Advancement of Psychiatry, a nonprofit tax exempt organization, is made possible largely through the voluntary contributions and efforts of its members. For their financial assistance during the past fiscal year, in helping it to fulfill its aims, GAP is grateful to the following foundations and organizations:

Sponsors

BING FUND
CIBA CORPORATION
MAURICE FALK MEDICAL FUND
GEIGY CHEMICAL CORPORATION
GENERAL SERVICE FOUNDATION
THE GRANT FOUNDATION
THE HOFFMANN-LA ROCHE FOUNDATION
SMITH KLINE & FRENCH FOUNDATION
TACONIC FOUNDATION
UPJOHN COMPANY
WALLACE LABORATORIES
WYETH LABORATORIES

Donors

CARRIER CLINIC
FOREST HOSPITAL FOUNDATION
GRALNICK FOUNDATION
MORRIS AND SOPHIE KARDON FOUNDATION
RIKER LABORATORIES

Publications of the
Group for the Advancement of Psychiatry

Because readers of this publication may not be aware of previously published GAP Reports and Symposiums, a selected listing of titles is given below.

"S" refers to Symposium

A complete listing of publications of the Group for the Advancement of Psychiatry may be obtained upon request from the Publications Office.

Bound volumes of Reports and Symposiums published since 1947 are also available. They include reports that are now out of print and unavailable in any other form.